Table of Contents

Contributors vii
Preface xv
Introduction xvii

Chapter 1: Are They an Adult Now?....................... 1
   How to support your increasingly independent student
   Shana Lee

Chapter 2: How Can They Balance It All? 7
   How to manage increasing expectations
   James M. Wright Jr.

Chapter 3: How Can I Help if My Student Is Feeling
          Burned Out? 15
   How to encourage motivation and focus
   Kerri Fowler

Chapter 4: Does a Major Even Matter? 23
   How to handle a late major change
   Melody Klein and Mel Cerra

Chapter 5: What Job Can You Get with That Major? 31
   How to narrow down career options
   Emily Pelkowski

Chapter 6: Who Will Take Care of You Overseas? 37
   How to make the most of their time abroad
   Jenny Sullivan

Chapter 7: You Want to Do More School? 49
   How to support the decision to attend graduate school
   Shanise N. Kent, Esq., MBA and Chelsea Petree, Ph.D.

Chapter 8: Can I See Your ID? 59
    How to talk about turning 21
    Ahmed Hosni

Chapter 9: There's Not an Office for That? 69
    How to advocate for resources after college
    Samantha Jeffries, LMFT

Chapter 10: Is This Relationship Serious? 79
    How to navigate increasingly romantic relationships
    Christine Self

Chapter 11: How Can My Child Transition from Student
       to Citizen? 87
    How to engage in the off-campus community
    Joshua Lee

Chapter 12: Is My Student Senior Ready? 95
    How to make the most of junior year
    Ashley Boltrushek

Conclusion 103

2025–2026 EDITION

COLLEGE JUNIOR READY

EXPERT ADVICE FOR PARENTS TO NAVIGATE THE JUNIOR YEAR OF COLLEGE

EDITED BY
CHELSEA PETREE, Ph.D.

A READY GUIDE

PARENT READY

PARENT READY.

2025–2026 Edition

Copyright © Parent Ready, Inc., 2025

Parent Ready supports the right to free expression and the value of copyright. The purpose of copyright is to encourage the creation of works that enrich our culture.

All rights reserved. No part of this book may be reprinted or reproduced in any form or by any electronic, mechanical, or other means, now known or hereafter invented, including photocopying, recording, and information storage and retrieval, without the prior written permission of the publisher, except in the case of brief quotations embodied in critical articles and reviews.

Published by Parent Ready, Inc.
8 East Windsor Avenue
Alexandria, Virginia 22301
https://parentready.com

Parent Ready and design are trademarks of Parent Ready, Inc.

The publisher is not responsible for websites (or their contents) that are not owned by the publisher.

ISBN: 979-8-9893392-6-6 (paperback)
ISBN: 979-8-9893392-7-3 (e-book)

Bulk purchases: Quantity discounts are available. Please make inquiries via https://collegeready.guide.

This book is dedicated to the parents, families, and caregivers of college juniors as you guide your student through the next chapter of their college experience.

Contributors

Editor

Chelsea Petree, Ph.D., is the Parent and Family Programs director at Rochester Institute of Technology (RIT). Chelsea moved to Rochester in 2015 to establish the Parent and Family Programs office, developing a comprehensive parent communications plan and implementing family events and engagement opportunities. She has worked to establish a "parents as partners" culture at RIT, increasing support of families across the institution. Chelsea received her Ph.D. in family social science from the University of Minnesota in 2013 and has served on the board of directors and as president of AHEPPP: Family Engagement in Higher Education. She has won several awards, including the 2019 Rising Alumni Award from the College of Education and Human Development at the University of Minnesota and the 2021 AHEPPP Powerful Partnership Award for Tiger Parent Project—a program that brings together RIT staff and faculty to learn more about the family experience and parent-student-university relationships. She is the editor of the *College Ready* book series.

Contributors

Ashley Boltrushek (any/all) works as the assistant dean of students at American University in Washington, DC. They hold a master of science in college student development and counseling and a bachelor of science in community health sustainability and education from the University of Massachusetts Lowell. Their primary role is to offer guidance to students managing acute and chronic physical and mental health concerns, particularly those who are preparing for or returning from hospitalization or temporary leave. Ash is passionate about destigmatizing mental health, empowering students to speak authentically about their experiences, and providing individualized student care and support. Ash is also deeply enthusiastic about: the Boston Bruins, family and friends, local coffee shops, art created by people they know, tattoos, museums, coffee-brewing gadgets, animal puns, board games, and tiny humans and dogs that belong to other humans.

Mel Cerra works as an academic advisor within the College of Business at Rochester. She holds a bachelor of arts in psychology from the State University of New York College at Geneseo and a master of science in school counseling from Canisius University. Prior to her work in higher education, Mel was a middle school, high school, and alternative education counselor for six years, supporting students and families in grades 5 through 12. She is passionate about building relationships to help students reach their full potential and engage with their campus and larger communities. In her personal life, Mel volunteers for the Alzheimer's Association of Rochester and serves in various capacities for Sigma Kappa sorority.

Kerri Fowler (she/her) serves as the director of Parents and Families Services at NC State, leading communication and programming efforts to engage parents from admissions through advancement. Before NC State, Kerri worked for the University of Vermont and Northern Vermont University at Lyndon (formerly known as Lyndon State College) in Enrollment Management. Kerri has served on the board of directors of AHEPPP: Family Engagement in Higher Education and is an active member of the organization. She received her master's degree in human development and organizational management from Springfield College and is working on her Ph.D. in higher education leadership, policy, and human development at NC State. Originally from the northeast corner of Vermont, Kerri relocated to the Raleigh area in 2012, where she resides with her husband, two daughters, and two rescue pups.

Ahmed Hosni is the assistant director of the Student Life Student Wellness Center at The Ohio State University and director of recovery at the Higher Education Center for Alcohol and Drug Misuse Prevention and Recovery. As a person in long-term recovery since 2007, his passion for supporting young people in or seeking recovery is personal. Ahmed's experience as a first-generation economically marginalized student pushes him to advocate for equitable and just processes and policies that provide all people with what they need to access education and culturally appropriate well-being resources. Ahmed received a bachelor of science in community, family, and addiction sciences from Texas Tech University—where he was a member of the Center for Collegiate Recovery Communities and president of the Association of Students About Service—and received his master's of social work from The Ohio State University. He is pursuing his Ed.D. in higher education and student affairs from The Ohio State University. Ahmed is grateful for the opportunity to serve as a board member of the Association of Recovery Schools and as a chairman of the board for the Association of Recovery in Higher Education.

Samantha Jeffries serves as the associate director of Student Case Management at Rochester Institute of Technology (RIT), where she helps students, parents, and families find resources and support services both on campus and within the Rochester community. She is a member of RIT's Student Behavior Consultation Team, which is tasked with coordinating resources and support for students of concern. In addition to her work at RIT, Samantha serves as a member of the Non-Clinical Case Manager Committee within the Higher Education Case Managers Association (HECMA). Her areas of focus in her work are mental health, crisis navigation, and community education. Prior to joining RIT, Samantha worked in community mental health, as well as within private practice and online telehealth platforms. She is a licensed marriage and family therapist (LMFT) in the State of New York and earned her bachelor's degree in psychology from the University of Rochester and her master of science in marriage and family therapy from the University of Rochester School of Medicine and Dentistry.

Shanise Kent is an assistant dean in the Graduate School and director of the Office of Professional, Adult & Continuing Knowledge at the University at Albany, State University of New York. She provides support, oversight, and advocacy for graduate programs, faculty, and students. Prior to joining the Graduate School at UAlbany in 2017, she was the director of Diversity Programs and Initiatives in the Thomas J. Watson College of Engineering and Applied Science at Binghamton University. During her 10 years at Binghamton, her work focused on supporting undergraduates interested in pursuing graduate education who were first-generation, low-income, and from historically underrepresented groups. Her experience includes assisting hundreds of students with all aspects of the graduate school application process. She holds a bachelor of arts in political science, a master's degree of business administration, and juris doctor (law degree) from the University at Buffalo, SUNY.

Melody Klein works as an academic advisor at Rochester Institute of Technology within the College of Business. She joined the RIT community in 2018 and has advised both the undergraduate and graduate student populations for several years. Her focus has always been to establish a holistic, positive, collaborative, and engaging relationship with her students during their time at RIT. She is passionate about supporting students in achieving their academic goals. Prior to her time at RIT, Melody worked at Ortho Clinical Diagnostics as a scientist and a user experience research analyst for over six years. She has also worked as a secondary science teacher and enjoyed bringing science to life in the classroom. Melody received her bachelor of science in biology and her master's degree in secondary science education. Her hobbies include traveling, spending time outdoors, staying active, camping and hiking with her family and dog, and being with her family of five.

Joshua Lee has dedicated his career to student growth and development, having served as assistant director of residence life, assistant dean of students, and junior class dean at St. Olaf College. Currently, as associate director of Alumni and Parent Relations, he continues to build community with the college for the mutual benefit of past, present, and future "Oles." In addition to higher education, his passions extend beyond the campus, serving his local community as an elected official. Joshua earned a master's in higher education at Grand Valley State University and bachelor of arts in earth sciences from Saint Cloud State University.

Shana Lee serves as the assistant dean of students and director for Parents and Families Engagement at Kent State University. In this role, she leads the Division of Student Life's efforts to incorporate parents and families as strategic partners in student success. As an employee with 30 years of experience, she has held several leadership roles working to build strategic opportunities, internally and externally, in alignment with university-level priorities. She also serves on the board of directors for AHEPPP: Family Engagement in Higher Education, is a member of the Equity, Belonging, and Inclusion Council, and is vice president for the Lower Midwest Regional Chapter of NADOHE (National Association of Diversity Officers in Higher Education). She earned a bachelor of science in communication studies from The Ohio State University, a master of arts in cultural foundations from Kent State University, and is pursuing an Ed.D. degree in interprofessional leadership at Kent.

Emily Pelkowski serves as director of Career Design and Outreach at Nazareth University, located in Rochester, New York, where she supervises a team of career coaches and collaborates with the Office of Community Engagement, Center for International Education, and the Professional Internship Program to provide meaningful experiential learning opportunities to her students. Emily has worked in the educational technology industry and with nonprofit global exchange programs. She owns a private career coaching practice, Thrive Career Coaching, where she supports clients with their career development. She earned a master of science in human development and family studies at the University of Rhode Island and a bachelor's degree in creative writing from St. John Fisher University.

Christine Self is the director of Parent & Family Relations at Texas Tech University and has worked in family engagement for over 20 years. She obtained her Ph.D. in higher education research at Texas Tech and enjoys researching family engagement, sexual violence prevention, and gender equity in higher education. Christine is the coeditor of *Engaging Families in Higher Education: Lessons Learned and Best Practices* (Routledge, 2023) and serves on the AHEPPP: Family Engagement in Higher Education board of directors.

Jenny Sullivan went overseas for the first time as a study abroad student to Harlaxton College in England through her undergraduate school, the University of Evansville. Her love of travel and learning about other cultures inspired her to earn her master's degree in higher education administration from Oregon State University. She has since lived in Ireland and Ecuador and has worked in international education for 14 years. She is the director of Education Abroad and International Fellowships at Rochester Institute of Technology in Rochester, New York.

James M. Wright Jr. works as the assistant director of Parent & Family Engagement at the University of Delaware. He holds a master's degree in higher education administration from Rowan University and a bachelor's degree in psychology from Stockton University. James has worked at various educational institutions throughout his career, with many of his previous work experiences in residence life and housing. He is passionate about helping students and families discover their purpose, which motivates and energizes him professionally. In his nonacademic life, he enjoys expressing his artistry in various ways, such as cooking, professional photography (under the username @theWrightAngle_), and part-time podcasting.

Preface

When I set out to begin this book, the last book written in the *College Ready* series, I thought it would be the most difficult to write. Is junior year really that special? First-year students are adjusting to all aspects of college life. Sophomores experience the "sophomore slump" and begin to find more independence. Seniors are preparing to say goodbye to their colleges and join the real world. But juniors? Isn't this the easiest year, where students have the college thing down but don't yet have to worry about the stress of the real world?

I reached out to my friends and colleagues and simply asked, "What makes junior year special?" It turns out, *a lot*. As I compiled their ideas with my own and outlined the chapters, I realized that this is, in fact, a unique year in a college student's life. The outline came together quickly and, as I read the drafts sent by my contributors, I learned a lot about what makes the third year of college special—and not as easy as I initially thought.

Preparing for post-college life begins junior year. Students study abroad, engage in the community, and find internships in their fields. Relationships become more serious, students hit the milestone of turning 21, and they become more independent in all aspects of their lives. They are showing more and more signs of the confident and mature adults they will become.

Not all experiences are positive, however. Students may experience serious burnout, as classes become more difficult and they take on leadership roles. They may have moments of doubt and question their choice of majors and careers, resulting in a late change. They begin to feel pressures related to senior year and post-college life. After working on this book, I now look around campus and see all this in my everyday interactions with students and parents. Junior year is filled with joy, hardship, and questions. It is a unique and incredible time in a student's college journey. And you, as parents and supporters, continue to play a role. The goal of this book is to help you understand the nature of junior year and to help you support your student through the ups, downs, questions, and triumphs.

I am lucky to have the opportunity to work with so many amazing people as the *College Ready* series grows. I am grateful for my publisher, Parent Ready, which cares so much about the parent experience—its books stretch across the middle, high school, and college years. A huge thank you to my copyeditor and to Anja Schmidt for keeping me on track. With each book, I am in awe of the contributors and the knowledge and dedication they bring to this series. I am lucky to have such amazing colleagues, and all the students and parents out there are lucky to have these amazing people at their campuses! A special shout-out to my friend Jenny, who stepped in at the final hour with great advice and the best attitude.

I will forever be grateful to AHEPPP: Family Engagement in Higher Education and the life-changing opportunities it has brought me. The things I learned and the ways in which I grew while leading this organization will always be reflected in my professional and personal lives.

To the parents, family members, and supporters: You make a difference. Your student needs you. We appreciate your partnership. We love seeing your relationship with your student grow. Your student will do amazing things because of you.

Chelsea Petree, Ph.D.
College Junior Ready Editor
Director, Parent and Family Programs
Rochester Institute of Technology

Introduction

This book is for the parents, family members, and others who are supporting their college student's increasing independence, while realizing that junior year will still bring questions and new challenges.

During the past two years, you have learned just as much about the college experience as your student. You are familiar with the resources offered to your student and to families. You understand when to step back and let your student lead and when to step in and offer greater levels of support. Your student is confident and mature and it feels like they need you less and less as time goes on. Junior year is sure to be a breeze, right?

The reality is that junior year is as unique as each of the other years in college, and what makes it more confusing is that every student in their junior year is in a different place. Some students will choose to move off campus, while others continue to appreciate the ease of living on campus. Some have stuck with their intended major from day one, while others are making a "late" change. Some are moving on to engagement opportunities in the community, while others are trying to catch every campus event and program, as those will soon come to end. Some are getting more serious with their significant others, while others choose to remain single and focus on their studies. This variability can make this year extra-challenging, as students have to make their own way and cannot compare their progress and success to their peers.

No matter their paths, however, juniors will share many experiences. Coursework becomes more demanding as students get deeper into their majors. Juniors need to think about post-college life, including decisions about attending graduate school and what experiences they need on their résumés to land a job. They are learning the need to prioritize and balance academics, real-life demands, future preparations, and self-care.

Your role as a supporter, cheerleader, and advocate will continue to evolve this year. As with the transition from first year to sophomore year, you will need to learn to step back and encourage your student to take responsibility for their decisions and actions. This sounds scary at first, but you will soon find yourself transitioning from parent-child relationship to a relationship of friends. Embrace it! Enjoy letting go and seeing your student thrive. Let them prove that they've got this. Let them succeed.

This book is written by professionals across the fields of family engagement, study abroad, case management, academic advising, student wellness, career services, and more. The content will help you support your student through this important year, including potential roadblocks, big milestones, and thoughts about post-college life. The conversation starters will help you bring up what can be challenging topics and have meaningful conversations around them.

Not all college students follow the same path, and there is not one right way to do college. While the content of this book reflects areas of interest typical for the junior year, your student may have already experienced some of these topics or may not encounter them at all. Every family is different, and parts of the book will resonate differently with each reader. Parents have many of their own experiences to contribute, and this book will provide perspective and guidance no matter your knowledge on each topic.

You are halfway there! This is junior year.

Chapter 1

ARE THEY AN ADULT NOW?

How to support your increasingly independent student

Shana Lee
Kent State University

Sophomore year is in the rearview mirror, while junior year is on the road ahead. Your student is now an upperclassman; however, there are still miles to go until they reach graduation. You have been on this journey as a copilot. You have hopefully engaged with your student's campus Parent and Family Program office, signed up for the family newsletter, attended parents and families weekends, or joined a parents council or two. Your student has probably turned to you for guidance and support, seeking to share many pivotal moments in their life thus far.

By now, most students have learned how to navigate the university system, gotten involved on campus, joined organizations, established friend groups who share their interests, and built relationships with faculty and staff. Your student may feel a sense of pride and accomplishment as they can finally engage in courses that align with their major, career interests, goals, and aspirations. As students solidify their

1

academic paths and become more confident, they may not lean on their parents as much. The number of daily phone calls may diminish. Instead of coming home during spring break, they may opt to participate in an alternative break experience, such as a service project with a friend. Junior year marks a period in the life of your student when they will begin to assert their independence and take complete control of the wheel.

Gaining independence and establishing their footing is key as they prepare for life after college. Building independence helps students manage, build, and maintain boundaries, take ownership, and learn to rely on themselves. However, this does not mean they will not need the assistance of family members from time to time. It simply means you will have to take the back seat and entrust your student with responsibility. As students begin to loosen ties to home, how can parents support their maturity and independence? Relax, relate, and release!

Relax, relate, release is a mantra popularized by Whitley Gilbert, a character in the late-1980s sitcom *A Different World*. In a discussion about the trials of life, Whitley's therapist instructs her to "relax, relate, and release!" You nurtured, protected, and supported your child from the start. You kissed their boo-boos and frightened away the monsters under the bed. Yielding responsibility to your student may be a different world experience, with bouts of trepidation and excitement. This is to be expected. However, practicing the relax, relate, and release mantra may strengthen the bond between you and your student and allow you both to enjoy this next phase of your lives.

Relax

Preparing for the unexpected in life can be scary. You are probably wondering whether your student is prepared and equipped to handle the responsibilities associated with the independence that comes with aging through college. Relax! They are prepared, or will be with more practice. Students are resourceful and have the skills and capabilities to find the answers. They've already been practicing this for two years by reaching out to their advisors, making their own doctor's appointments, putting themselves out there by joining a club or team, and living (more or less) independently from you. Additionally, by their junior year, most students have established a network of friends and resources that can offer support and guidance. It is normal for juniors to begin to rely more on their campus network than their home network. If this isn't the case with your student, it's time you encourage them to start. Encourage them to connect with people on campus—staff, faculty, and peers—and begin to build their network.

It is natural to want to hold onto the steering wheel as long as possible, but when parents only focus on what there is to lose, they miss out on what can be gained. Letting go and relaxing does not mean you do not care. It signals that you empower your student to embrace their freedom and that you trust them to make the right decisions.

Trust and independence go hand in hand. When a person feels they are trusted, they are more likely to live up to the expectations set for them. They have a clear understanding of their capabilities and skills and seek help when needed. Trust that your student can handle pretty much anything that comes their way. Have faith in the values you instilled in your student and find comfort in knowing that they will consult you in their time of need. Relax!

Relate

Junior year will be a year of focus and change. No matter a person's background and path, change is constant and sometimes difficult to manage. Grant your student some grace, sprinkled with encouragement. Remember what it was like when you were at a crossroads in your life. If you had someone who provided a listening ear, did not judge, and encouraged you to take a leap of faith, provide that for your student.

By junior year, your student will be immersed in their core major courses and planning for the future. Encourage them to begin planting seeds now for how they envision life beyond college. Have them share with you their thoughts regarding the next steps, be it a job, graduate school, or something else, and nudge them to act. Relate to them by acknowledging that it is natural to be excited and fearful of the unknown. Share your own experiences of when you went through a big change (related to college or not). What were your fears and hesitations? How did you overcome them? What was the result?

Connecting with your student in this phase requires a shift in parenting from a parent-child relationship to viewing and embracing them as an adult. It also requires communication and ensuring they feel heard and understood. Fostering independence includes motivating them to act with intention and inspiring them to achieve the goals they have set for themselves. This will help them to develop critical thinking, make confident decisions, and solve problems along the way. Relating to your student simply means being open to the possible, listening, and supporting. You may not always agree with your student, and that is okay. They will listen to your advice and take it into consideration, but they need to start making major life decisions on their own. You will always serve as a critical support base for them. Relate!

Release

The act of releasing can be therapeutic. There is a sensation of calmness and deep relaxation after a massage, for example, where the tension you once felt in your neck or lower back has been released. You now feel like a new person, as though you can walk on air. This feeling of release should happen with both you and your student this year. Your student has learned a lot in the past couple years and is ready to continue to grow with your support, but they no longer need your control. This might be scary, but it should also feel good, as you are able to let go of this stress and focus on other areas of your life.

As for your student—give them a confidence boost through your release of control by showing them you believe in them. They will feel empowered if they know you have faith in their abilities and capabilities as an adult. There may be a time or two when you want to intervene. Try to grant them space to uncover solutions to the challenges they are experiencing. The power of choice can evoke rich learning experiences and lead to meaningful life experiences. Release!

Closing Advice

Is your junior an adult now? In most ways, yes. But they will still need and want your advice and support. You will likely see a big spike in independence in your student this year, and that should excite you! The transition into a parent-child relationship that feels more like a friendship can be fun. As you learn to let go and empower your student to take the wheel, remember to relax, relate, and release!

Conversation Starters

- In what areas of your life (e.g., academics, self-care, real-world living) are you feeling the most confident and independent?
- In what areas of your life do you feel like you still need my support?
- How can I best support you through your junior year?
- How can I know when you just want me to listen and when you want advice?
- How do you intend to balance academics and other responsibilities? Are there ways in which I can offer advice to assist you in prioritizing?

Chapter 2
HOW CAN THEY BALANCE IT ALL?

How to manage increasing expectations

James M. Wright Jr.
University of Delaware

Junior year can be an absolute blast for your student, filled to the brim with exciting experiences and unforgettable memories. It's a time of growth, exploration, and self-discovery that will shape their future in countless ways. Many students have a sense of where they need to improve as they enter their junior year. By now, they have formed friendships in class, clubs, organizations, or at work. They have also found mentors who have helped them navigate their college experience so far—like a professor who might have assisted them with tough coursework or an advisor who is offering career advice. It's likely they have faced some challenges along the way, as most students do. No matter their previous experiences, junior year is crucial to their success, and they are realizing the pressure to do well.

Your student has been at their university for a couple years now, so on the one hand, they feel like an old pro. They are familiar with campus, know the best places to eat, and have already discovered the good study spots. On the other hand, they are approaching graduation, and they might feel like they need to focus on the unknowns of post-college life. They will need to balance these feelings, as well as increased academic pressure, career or graduate school preparation, and more active social lives.

Your junior may feel like they are between two different worlds as they strive to make the most of this year and fill any gaps in their academic, social, or personal lives, while looking ahead to life after graduation. Finding balance can be challenging, but with the right support, it is certainly achievable. This chapter will outline some crucial ways you can help your student balance everything and find motivation to successfully complete their junior year.

Coursework Excellence

At this stage of your student's college journey, they probably know which courses require more effort and which ones they can manage with less time investment. If your student enjoys their core classes but doesn't find the general ones appealing, that's perfectly fine. At this stage, they have greater freedom to take courses that spark their interest, even outside of their major. They can use general education credits to dig into a personal interest or learn something just for fun. By seeking classes they are interested in, they will have greater motivation to excel in their coursework.

As your student progresses through their college experience, their core courses become more challenging. Your student may get overwhelmed if they missed something or cannot connect what they learned in their last core course to this one. Daily homework and reading will take more time. Overall, they will have more to balance on the academic side. As they deal with this new level of coursework, as well as increased pressure to do well, there are a number of resources that will support them, including tutors and advisors.

There are different types of tutors available to help students with their studies. Some tutors specialize in general writing and math, which can be helpful to identify and fill any gaps in these subject areas. Other tutors focus on the major the student is studying and can assist with the core course content materials related to that program. Even if your student has not used a tutor in the past, they should not hesitate to reach out to one now if needed.

Academic advisors can help your student understand their course load and provide guidance on how to manage it effectively. Hopefully at this point your student has interacted with their advisor, but it is common to not have mandatory advising meetings in a student's junior and senior years. Even if appointments aren't mandatory, academic advisors are happy to continue to meet through a student's entire college career.

Student Success and Community Engagement

Since the first day of college, students seek out new social circles and friendships. Fortunately, the college experience provides many opportunities to meet new people. If your student is part of a club or organization on campus, they probably have a dedicated friend group they can rely on. They may have developed relationships with classmates in the same program or major. Regardless of how they made friends, your student will realize their relationships can be the first step in building a network of reliable personal and professional contacts whom they can trust.

While struggling to balance academic responsibilities, it can be challenging to maintain or strengthen friendships. Additionally, friendships will continue to shift as students move to new housing and make new priorities about academics and campus involvement. It is normal to continue to make new friends throughout college and for some friendships to begin to fade. What is important is that, however big or small, your student has a support system that can provide guidance on this journey.

Your student should engage with their campus community just as much as they surround themselves with good company. During their junior year, students often increase their involvement by taking on leadership roles within campus organizations. They may also finally have the confidence to put themselves out there and try a new hobby by joining a club. They may see the approach of their senior year as a good reason to take advantage of more campus events and activities. Whatever the case, it's a lot to balance. It may be necessary for your junior to narrow down their engagements, make priorities, and focus on what truly matters to them. Although they might want to do everything, as they progress through their junior year, it might not be feasible as coursework gets harder and pressures to prepare for the future increase. They should aim to develop and nurture their relationships, enhance their leadership skills, and gain new skills that will help them become a well-rounded student and a successful future professional in a way that seems manageable.

Preparing for the Future

Preparing for the future is daunting at any time. Luckily, juniors have the advantage of more time. Proper preparation is crucial for a student's success in the professional world. This is the time for juniors to start exploring internship and graduate school options.

Graduate school is an excellent option for students wanting to specialize in a specific area. It provides an opportunity to stay immersed in the college experience while working on research, capstone projects, or other areas of interest, depending on the field. Additionally, graduate schools offer another network of students and professionals to continue to learn from. Students considering graduate school will need to begin preparing in their junior year (see Chapter 7 for details on graduate school).

Internships provide access to real-world professional opportunities. Many students start thinking about and working in internships around their junior year. Some students prefer internships in their field so they can start to build a foundation of professionals who understand their journeys. Others choose internships that offer the chance to experience a specific culture, style, or setting in their fields.

Considering graduate school and internship experiences is important during junior year, adding even more for your student to balance. While this may feel intimidating, there are many resources on campus, and students have options—they only need to take the opportunities that are right for them.

Self-Care is the Best Care

Who doesn't love an ice-cold lemonade on the beach while listening to the waves crash? Or hiking a couple of miles to just clear your mind? Whatever the type of break, taking one can help tremendously, especially during a stressful junior year.

Encourage your junior to **exercise**, helping them to focus on something other than their day-to-day work. The gym can be a home to students who are not just looking to bulk up, but also to remain active throughout the day. Hiking is a good way for students to get outdoors, spend time with friends, and challenge themselves in a different way than solely relying on the gym.

Daily journaling can help students see progress from start to finish on a given emotion, task, or moment in life. Trying to balance everything can be stressful, but writing things down can ease that stress. Daily gratitude also helps, because sometimes we forget everything we could be thankful for when we are presented with stressful situations. So, writing down or repeating a specific affirmation such as, "I am grateful for my friends," "I am happy because today is the day I get to go to my favorite campus program," or "I am thankful for all of the opportunities my professors gave me throughout my time at this institution," can be helpful.

Exercise and journaling are just two examples of ways students can make time for the things they enjoy. Whatever their form of release, help your student understand that, no matter how busy they are and how tough it is to balance everything, prioritizing breaks and self-care is essential to success.

Closing Advice

Achieving balance doesn't just happen during junior year; it's a continuous process. Encouraging your student to pursue their passions, take on leadership opportunities, and cultivate a sense of belonging is crucial to their growth and development—but remind them to practice self-care. Support your student's experiences and empathize with their struggles. Doing so helps create an environment that fosters growth and inspires them to excel in all aspects of their life.

Conversation Starters

- What electives are you taking this year? Did you find classes that fit a personal interest?
- When do you plan to meet with your academic advisor this year?
- How will you balance your increased academic workload?
- What extracurricular activities will you continue with this year? Do you plan to try any new ones?
- How are you making time for your friends this year?
- What do you do when you need to take a break or relax?

Chapter 3
HOW CAN I HELP IF MY STUDENT IS FEELING BURNED OUT?

How to encourage motivation and focus

Kerri Fowler
North Carolina State University

It is normal for students to experience burnout and exhaustion during their junior year of college and, in many ways, it should be anticipated. Junior year is the equivalent of the halfway marker in a marathon. It's the point where one has come too far to return to the start, but one isn't quite close enough to see the finish line. It's where the body and the mind begin to conflict. Feelings of self-doubt can be paired with a lack of focus, motivation, and stamina. The good news is that you can help by understanding what's going on with your student and why.

Why Is This Happening Now?

Whether running a race or working toward a college degree, hitting the midway point is hard. Mental and physical exhaustion are key indicators of psychosomatic expression. In other words, when the mind becomes tired, we lose focus. Losing focus can cause frustration, anxiety, and a loss of momentum, all of which compromise one's will, determination, and motivation.

Mental exhaustion sends the mind into overdrive, which quickly misfires and takes over all rational emotions, logic, and even physical ability. Feelings of self-doubt creep in, followed by a myriad of questions that begin to risk one's confidence. *Why am I here? What am I doing? What did I get myself into?* Thoughts of quitting replace thoughts of success...*I should just be done. It's not worth it. It's not like I'm going to win anything. No one's even around, I could just cut the course and be done. Who really cares anyway?*

At the midpoint of their college experience, your student may be asking themselves questions such as these. The good news is that this is perfectly normal, and it doesn't have to be difficult to get back on track. Being aware of this struggle and knowing how to look out for greater issues is key to supporting your student through this year.

Signs Your Student is Experiencing Burnout

The following are some of the common warning signs that students who are facing burnout often show. It is important to note that every student is unique, so if your student has experienced difficulties in the past, it does not necessarily mean they will experience the same challenges again. Be careful not to react too quickly or dismiss their experiences.

Academic withdrawal

With some, this type of struggle is easy to identify. For example, high-achieving students who have suddenly shifted their energies so they have little to no interest in academics or cocurricular activities and are making a habit of missing classes and assignments are perhaps the easiest to identify—but don't be fooled. There is a spectrum of burnout, and it has nothing to do with how connected or close to your student you are. As a parent, you may not know if your student is withdrawing in this way. Using open-ended questions and listening to what your student is saying will help you understand if their motivation has shifted.

Physical ailments

For some students, junior year burnout manifests physically with few or even no academic effects. Headaches, nausea, anxiety, depression, rapid weight loss or weight gain, a lack of healthy hygiene habits, loss of interest in passions or activities, unusual irritability, insomnia, or the opposite hypersomnia are all potential symptoms of burnout. If your student is constantly sick or can't seem to shake that one cold or illness for weeks on end, they may be on the brink of burnout.

Avoidance or denial

Students have acquired more knowledge than just how to make the grade. Many have learned how to hide their pain, stress, and lingering doubt. Parents and family members tend to blame themselves or even put up a wall, thinking, "My student would tell me." Perhaps they will, but more often than not, the truth is that your student doesn't want to disappoint you, especially if they know you have a financial investment in their future. This is why it is critical to check in with your student often.

The Power of a Check-In

Checking in with your student is critical to supporting their success and can look different for everyone. Whether it's a Sunday night phone call, a twice weekly text, or something less structured, checking in with your student is not checking up on them. Avoid asking about tests and assignments or whether they remembered to take their vitamins; instead, let your check-ins be reminders of support. Take interest in what's new, who their friends are, what clubs or organizations they are interested in, or what game they might go to that week. Check-ins remind your student that you're thinking of them and that you are their biggest cheerleader. Give them space and time to respond, but also mix it up. If you and your student tend to be text-heavy, give them a phone call. If you talk frequently but haven't seen your student in a while, set up a time to video chat.

Use check-ins to celebrate the wins, large and small, and to glean how your student is doing. Students facing burnout tend to live in a world of worry. Even after a victory, they tend to be worried about what's next: the next test, the next assignment, the next hurdle. They are acutely aware of every potential roadblock in their path, and it often overshadows the little and big accomplishments. If it sounds heavy, that's because—for your student—it is. However, heavy doesn't mean that it can't be worked through. You can be a major resource and support system.

Tips for Supporting Your Student

To help your student persevere and regain the mental strength to keep going and push through the junior year burnout, here are some practical measures you can take:

Unlock your inner champion

More than a fan, a champion is a powerful voice of reason and influence. Champions are typically the ones we hear in the background, motivating us and believing in us when we don't always believe in ourselves. Champions know when to push and when to let things be. They are a routine check-in, a voice of reason, and the proper perspective that can help a student recalibrate when they are feeling overwhelmed. As a champion, it is your role to routinely check in with your student. Give them permission to refuel, rest, and reset as needed, and encourage them.

Be strategic

Strategy is key when communicating with evolving adults. It's often not *what* you ask, it's *how* you ask. Here are some tips for navigating conversations (whether difficult or easy) with your college student:

- Approach conversations with a nonjudgmental tone.
- Keep your opinion to yourself. If you feel compelled to share, ask, "Do you want my opinion, or would you just like me to listen?"
- Don't compare their situation to yourself, to your neighbor's student, to your other children, to your hairdresser's niece twice removed…just don't do it. Comparison will only dilute any point you are trying to make. Your student's experience, even if common, is unique to them, and using any comparison, even to help normalize the situation, will only make them feel small.
- Use open-ended questions. Questions that begin with "how," "why," or "what" or phrases such as "tell me more about…" leave more opportunity for a conversational response rather than a one-word answer.

Encourage them to start small

Many students experience burnout and can feel overwhelmed by their workload. It can be helpful to advise them to focus on the present moment and break down their tasks into smaller, more manageable parts. Suggest they make a list, because the work might not seem as intimidating when written down and checked off. The proverb,

"How do you eat an elephant? One bite at a time," reminds us that even the most daunting tasks can be tackled gradually. Students who are struggling may not know where to start, so offering guidance can be beneficial.

Be consistent but not constant

There is a major difference between the two. Being consistent means that you have prioritized time to check in with your student. If you ask how they are doing and they brush you off, give it time, and then revisit the question. Perhaps rephrase it or try a different strategy. Being constant is the approach that is often referred to as nagging. Avoid asking the same question over and over or calling and texting multiple times throughout day or even week. Be respectful of your student's schedule and their priorities, but don't relinquish support.

Know the resources

Colleges and universities have a wide variety of resources available to students to help support personal and academic success. The likelihood of your student having heard about the resources is strong, but (a) understanding how these resources can help them and (b) taking advantage of them may not be as likely. Take time to research the programs at your student's institution to learn more about what might be a good fit, and then communicate with your student about their options. Avoid reaching out directly to the resources on behalf of your student, but talk to your student about how they can advocate for themselves. The exception to this general guideline: If your student is experiencing or expressing symptoms of depression, thoughts of harm to self or others, or suicide, reach out to public safety or emergency resources, or file a student concern report so those nearby can provide immediate assistance and support.

Be a fan

Sometimes there is no greater feeling than the moment you see, hear, or feel someone rooting for you. Having a special individual who believes you can do it and is cheering you on no matter what can push someone through some of the hardest physical and mental barriers. *You* are your student's biggest cheerleader and all-time #1 fan. Your love and support are not only needed at orientation and again at commencement, but also at every step of the way. Particularly when they don't believe in themselves, they will most certainly need you to.

Closing Advice

If your student is experiencing burnout, remember the wide array of institutional resources available to support students. Don't be afraid to explore the various options and encourage your student to take advantage of them. If you're unsure where to turn, keep in mind that there are also programs available to support parents and families, usually found on the institution's website. Don't hesitate to reach out for help. These resources can be a valuable tool for you and your student to navigate this challenging time and get back on track.

Conversation Starters

- How are you feeling about your classes this semester?
- How often are you feeling stressed?
- Why do you think you are feeling this way?
- What does your daily routine look like?
- I see how hard you're working and I'm so proud of you, but it's important to take time for yourself. What are you doing for fun?
- Let's talk through what's causing you the most stress and see what your options might be.
- How can I help?
- Have you thought about talking to a [counselor, advisor, mentor, etc.]?

Chapter 4
DOES A MAJOR EVEN MATTER?

How to handle a late major change

Melody Klein and Mel Cerra
Rochester Institute of Technology

By their junior year, your student has most likely had significant exposure to major-specific coursework and skill-building. Ideally, they have a strong sense of the career paths that their program can lead to. However, there is variability in students making these connections, depending on their level of maturity and self-awareness. At this level, your student will often be very engaged with faculty and peers in their program because they are participating in clubs, getting to know faculty in classes and at college events (such as seminars and educational talks), and engaging with peers in and out of class.

By their junior year, many students have completed or are looking for a cooperative education (co-op) or internship opportunity within their program's focus. A co-op or internship allows students the chance to see what the career options within their field are and what the day-to-day work looks like. They will have the chance to practice and hone skills learned in the classroom in a real-world setting, as well as work with those in the industry with years of experience. They also may have learned something or made a new connection that sparked their interest in a different field. Their current major may have lost some of its charm and expectation isn't lining up with reality. A panic (or excitement!) may be setting in now that college is nearing completion and the real world is next! *Now what?*

So, while it may be uncommon for a third-year student to be considering a program change, it does happen. Here's what to consider when it does.

Does a Major Even Matter?

Does a major matter? It depends. An undergraduate major does matter when it comes to specialized career paths. Let's consider the medical field. A student applying to medical school and sitting for the MCAT would be lost without a strong background in biology, chemistry, physics, psychology, and sociology. Not only will this knowledge affect their exam score, which opens or closes the door to medical school admission, but they also need to be prepared to compete academically. Or, consider a student who wants to work as an accountant. Without content knowledge and course-specific credit hours, they would not qualify to sit for the CPA (certified public accountant) Exam, which is the gateway for a career as a certified public accountant.

For other career paths, an undergraduate major is not necessarily the deciding factor in a student's prospects for employment. As working adults, we know that it's not always the degree that makes someone successful in their career. A student's experiences in college lay the foundation for job skills, such as learning how to communicate effectively, problem-solving across settings, advocating for themselves, and working effectively as part of a team. Also important to future employers is engagement in extracurriculars such as athletics, clubs/organizations, part-time employment, and co-ops/internships, as these showcase leadership and time-management skills, personality, passions, and real-world knowledge.

While a major may matter, parents can work with their students to identify and connect with resources to help explore alternate options.

The Option of Graduate School

If your student is looking to transition to another field, a graduate degree can be a great opportunity to move toward a new career field in some situations. Encourage your student to review admissions requirements and program curricula. Many graduate programs are flexible with an undergraduate major if a student can show their enthusiasm for the field and success on entrance examinations such as the GRE, GMAT, or LSAT. If those exams seem daunting, encourage your student to seek out preparatory courses and workbooks. Positive recommendations from their current faculty, supervisors, and advisors can indicate to graduate admissions offices that this student has what it takes to be successful. Once they have the required test scores, applications, letters of reference, and personal statement, the door may be open to gain the content knowledge specific to this new field of interest. Many graduate programs also require internship experiences that will build their résumé and professional network. By the end of a graduate program, an undergraduate *major* (but not the degree and experience of those undergraduate years) becomes a footnote in their story.

How to Change Majors

Here are some practical considerations if your student has decided that a change of major is needed:

Reflect with your student

This can be a great time to reflect with your student about how and why you landed in your own profession(s). As suggested in Chapter 1, relate! Ask what your student is feeling and what has led them to strongly consider a major change. Also, what are they looking for in a new program? Have they identified one or more programs they would like to pursue?

Once they can identify what they are looking for, it's a perfect time to research options. They can do this by working with an academic advisor, career counselor, faculty mentors, peers, or alumni, or by attending workshops and talks. Attending these meetings having done prior research into the major/career option they are now considering, along with what they want to learn about the program or career, will only enhance the conversation and help your student extract the information they are seeking. Ideally, they will prepare a list of questions before these meetings, such as:

- How many additional classes would I need if I change to this new major?
- How much longer would I need to stay beyond when I thought I would be graduating?
- What are the career options for this major and the hiring outlook for those jobs?
- What does the change of major process entail?
- Are there GPA or prerequisite requirements to change to this major?
- Other than a major, are there minors, certifications, and experiences that I can tap into?

Job shadowing in the prospective field can be a useful tool as well. It can help your student determine how a new career might fit. It is a great opportunity to meet professionals in the industry and ask questions such as :

- What led you to this career?
- What do you love about it?

- What don't you love about it?
- What does a "day in the life" look like?

Consider viability

Working with an academic or faculty advisor can allow your student to map out an academic timeline for the proposed shift in program. They will need to identify if there is prerequisite coursework that must be completed to make this change. And what else does the major change process entail? Is there availability within the new program? Once more is known about the proposed major change, your student should meet with a financial aid advisor to determine additional cost, if any, that may be incurred from the change. In the end, your student should be able to answer these questions:

- Is this change warranted?
- Do the benefits outweigh the cost of a change, whether that cost is time or money?
- If they do not change their major, can they still find jobs within their desired field or be admissible to a graduate program to achieve their career goal?

Closing Advice

Junior year is typically when reality sets in. After just one more year of college, your student is expected to start a career in the field of their major. They've likely gained content-specific knowledge in their upper-level courses, developed mentors through faculty connections, and may have done an internship or job shadow that clarified career prospects. But if they have ever had doubts, now is the time when those doubts may get louder. While it can be frustrating, concerning, and confusing to help your student navigate a change of major later in their college career, not every journey is linear. The bumps in the road, detours, and delays often provide important life lessons. This can be an opportunity for your student to sit with uncertainty and evaluate their decision-making process without acting prematurely. Stay open-minded and ask open-ended questions. Steer your student toward on-campus resources. Together, map out the different avenues your student can take to arrive at their desired outcome, whether they change their major or not.

Conversation Starters

- Have you met with a career counselor for guidance and to do a career assessment?
- What research have you done into the change-of-major process?
- Who can you talk to on campus about the pros and cons of changing majors?
- What experiences outside the classroom can help you gain knowledge/skills in a different field?
- Are there nonnegotiables you need to follow this new path (e.g., GPA, graduate degrees, certification exams, specific courses)?
- Have you job shadowed in the new field of interest? Have you read job descriptions within this field? Does the real-world nature of the career line up with your expectations?
- What are the current and future job market projections for this field?
- What are your contingency plans if you cannot change majors?
- How can you market yourself on your résumé and cover letter to make use of the skills and experiences already in your toolbox? Which skills and strengths are transferable across different job types?

Chapter 5

WHAT JOB CAN YOU GET WITH THAT MAJOR?

How to narrow down career options

Emily Pelkowski
Nazareth University

While some students select majors that lead directly to a specific career path, such as nursing, education, or engineering, many other students opt to major in subjects that are much broader in scope and can lead to a variety of career options. For example, a psychology major could certainly end up working as a psychologist but could just as likely end up working in another role entirely. Further, lots of today's jobs do not have a directly correlated undergraduate major. This chapter will cover ways to help your student narrow down career options from a broad major and consider how to make the best and most informed career choices.

Interests, Skills, and Values

Deciding on a major/career can be one of the most stressful aspects of college. Most colleges and universities require students to declare a major before junior year, but that's only one piece of the puzzle. What if your student has decided on a broad major, like business or English? How can you help your student translate their major into a sustainable, meaningful career? First, it's important for your student to **identify their interests**. What classes do they most enjoy? What interests does your student have outside the classroom? How do they spend their downtime? You can brainstorm together the industries, companies, or job functions that most closely align with these interests. If you're unsure about where to look, the Bureau of Labor Statistics has an excellent online resource called the "Occupational Outlook Handbook" (bls.gov/ooh), which provides insight into various occupations, median incomes for those jobs, and valuable information for researching them.

Next, **think about the skills** that your student possesses, both the ones they naturally have and those that can be learned and developed. Start with what skills your student's coursework, jobs, internships, and volunteer experiences have helped them to develop. Once your student has identified their strongest skill sets (e.g., communications, computer literacy, critical thinking, research and data analysis, or writing), you can help them identify which careers would best match. Many employers use skill-based hiring practices, focusing on specific skills instead of education and prior experience. Your student should be prepared to talk beyond their experiences and be able to share what skills and talents they have and how those skills contribute to a job.

Lastly, what matters most to your student? An essential component of career exploration is **understanding the role that values play** in an individual's satisfaction with their work. For example, some people value high levels of flexibility and autonomy, while others seek accountability and structure. Other common values include collaboration, creativity, stability, and achievement. If you know that your student values creativity, for example, they might be more satisfied in their career if there are opportunities to be creative. Knowing the importance of combining interests, values, and skills can make deciding on a job a lot easier.

Experiential Learning

The best way to figure out what your student may like (and what they don't—which is just as important!) is by doing. Certain majors and programs build experiential learning opportunities into the curriculum. Common examples include student teaching for education majors and clinical rotations for nursing majors. While it's important to note that most of these required experiences don't begin until junior year, it's equally important to know that many majors and/or universities do not have experiential learning requirements at all. If your student's major doesn't require experiential learning, it is highly beneficial to consider finding at least one opportunity to connect classroom learning to the real world through an experience. Career exploration can come from volunteerism, internships, part-time jobs (on or off campus), and co-ops. It's hard to know for sure if a job is right for your student until they have a chance to do it, and college is the perfect place to test-drive careers through various forms of experiential learning. These experiential learning opportunities provide value by serving as a tool for career exploration. They are also great résumé builders.

Career Conversations

Another excellent way to learn about career options is to talk to people about the work they do. Students can tap into the college alumni network—through LinkedIn or the alumni engagement office—to explore what types of jobs are held by people who graduated with their major. You can also connect your student with your professional network, which can help provide knowledge and potential opportunities. Your student should ask questions like:

- What does a typical workday look like for you?
- What classes and experiences best prepared you for your current job?
- What do you like most/least about your work?
- What advice do you have for a student who is interested in doing what you do?

Another way to gain opportunities for career conversations is to join professional organizations (e.g., the National Association of Social Workers). Student memberships are usually inexpensive, and there are many opportunities to network and learn from other members about their career journeys. Some professional organizations offer free or discounted webinars, local meetups, regional conferences, or mentoring programs, all of which are excellent ways to learn more about career opportunities.

Preparing for Life After Graduation

If your student decides to pursue a career that requires graduate school, junior year is when students typically begin taking entrance exams (e.g., LCAT, MCAT, GRE) and applying for admission. For students who aren't sure what they want to do, though, going to graduate school is a really expensive way to figure it out. Look into postgraduate service opportunities, such as AmeriCorps or Peace Corps, to build additional skills, develop a professional network, and add meaningful experience to their résumé. If they are not interested in postgraduate service, there are many other jobs that can serve as a great first step in applying your student's interests, skills, and values. The first full-time position post-college isn't likely to be a dream job, but it can certainly provide experience, knowledge, and professional connections. Encourage your student to take advantage of the campus career center to help with developing their résumé and other professional documents and starting the job search. Remind your student that job searching is a job in and of itself, so there's no shame in waiting until after graduation to dive headfirst into the process if this is a financial option.

Closing Advice

Deciding what to do with your major—especially if it's a broad topic—can be challenging. However, by exploring options, researching various career paths, and participating in experiential learning opportunities, the decision will be a lot easier to make. Remember, the first job out of college is not likely to be the perfect fit or a dream job, but every opportunity is a stepping stone to the next.

Conversation Starters

- What is the most interesting part of your major?
- What academic topics interest you most outside of your major?
- What values matter most to you in a future career?
- What are some experiential learning opportunities you can explore? What support for internships or co-ops is available to you?
- What are the most common jobs that people get with your major?

Chapter 6

WHO WILL TAKE CARE OF YOU OVERSEAS?

How to make the most of their time abroad

Jenny Sullivan
Rochester Institute of Technology

By junior year, many students are feeling confident in their majors and settled into campus life. Now they might be ready to take on a new challenge through study abroad. After a year of organizing finances, aligning coursework, and applying for visas and passports, the bags are packed and it is time to say goodbye. You know this will be a great experience for your student, but as the departure date approaches, you may find yourself wondering, *did we make the right choice? Will my student be okay?* This chapter will explore some of the experiences your student might encounter while they are abroad and ways that you can support them.

Adapting to a New Environment

The first challenge your student will experience when studying abroad is adapting to their new environment. In the 1980s, Young Yun Kim's research on cultural adaptation outlined four stages that a person experiences in a new cultural setting, which your student may experience while abroad:

- **Honeymoon stage:** Everything is new and exciting. Your student is energized by a sense of adventure.

- **Negotiation:** The excitement is wearing off and your student might feel frustrated, irritated, and sad. Everyday experiences like eating breakfast and commuting to school are challenging.

- **Adjustment:** The emotional roller coaster is starting to level off. Your student will have good and bad days, but they are building routines, meeting people, and things are starting to click.

- **Mastery:** Your student is comfortable in their new environment. They are understanding and adapting to cultural nuances. They might be feeling like a local and may even contemplate not wanting to return home.

Culture shock is the positive and negative feelings, including homesickness, that your student will experience when they enter a completely new environment and explore new ways of doing and being. The length and severity of a student's culture shock can depend on things like the length of the program, how different the host culture is, and previous experience with travel and language. It can also be exacerbated by common travel experiences like jet lag, diet changes, time changes, and stress/anxiety. Culture shock can last for a few days or a few months and, in extreme cases, can lead to depression. Fortunately, there are several effective strategies for managing culture shock and homesickness:

- **Do research before departure.** It's important to read articles, listen to podcasts, and talk to people who've traveled before. The more your student's expectations align with reality, the less shock they will experience. Many university study abroad offices have peer mentors or global ambassadors to share insights.

- **Reflect on and recognize feelings.** Keeping a journal or talking to others going through a similar experience is a great way for students to cope. If they can identify what they are experiencing, they can apply strategies to combat it. Sharing also helps them realize they are not alone and strengthens their support network.

- **Manage expectations.** Students often choose study abroad as a way to step outside of their comfort zone. They are doing this because they know that the greatest growth and most profound change comes from being challenged and learning to be resilient and adaptable. Your encouragement can be empowering.

- **Take a break.** Remind your student that it's okay to step back and take comfort in something familiar. Maybe that means calling home or finding the nearest McDonald's for lunch. Taking baby steps out of their comfort zone and accomplishing minor goals builds confidence and leads to great accomplishments in the long term.

If none of these strategies are effective and the situation becomes extreme (e.g., your student is not eating, not attending class, isolating), it is very important that they seek help from their study abroad provider or local mental health provider. In the worst-case scenario, your student could return home temporarily or permanently.

Things to Consider During an Overseas Program

While your student is traveling abroad, they may encounter challenges in navigating local systems. Most students are required to participate in a predeparture workshop given by their study abroad offices and on-site orientation sessions by faculty and in-country providers that help them manage these challenges. Awareness of the potential areas below will help you prepare your student for what to expect and start to develop their confidence.

Safety

While abroad, it is important that your student is vigilant and aware of their surroundings. Americans often stand out and, as a result, could be targets for petty crime. Your student should follow the U.S. State Department's guide on travel warnings and register for the federal government's Smart Traveler Enrollment Program (STEP, step.state.gov), which provides localized security alerts and assistance to American citizens in an emergency abroad. Your student should take precautions like never traveling alone, knowing the emergency services number, and learning how to say "help" in the local language.

Managing physical and mental health

If your student has a health condition, it's important that they inform their health care provider so they can develop a plan for managing their health while abroad. Most study abroad providers will supply international health insurance for your student, which will help them identify local providers who speak English and cover costs. If your student is on medication, ensure that it is legal in the host country. Your student should try to bring enough for the whole trip, with some extra in case flights are canceled/delayed. Carry medications in carry-on luggage in case checked luggage gets lost, and keep all medications in the original packaging so ingredients and dosages are clear in case it needs to be replaced locally.

Identity abroad

Students with particular identities might face additional challenges abroad. For example, members of the LGBTQ+ community might not find all cultures or communities welcoming. BIPOC students might feel like they stand out and attract attention, or vice versa. Students should research local attitudes and identify resources at their home campus and in their host country to support them, if necessary.

Students with disabilities

Prior to traveling abroad, it's important that students with disabilities research cultural perspectives related to their disability, clearly communicate their needs to their study abroad provider or host university, and develop a plan for managing their access needs. Once in-country, it is essential that they maintain communication with their support network so services can be realigned, if necessary.

Romantic relationships

Your student may find themselves developing a close relationship with a local or someone else on the program. It is important that they understand the cultural norms of the host country as pertains to things like dating, displays of affection, consent, etc. Like they do at home, your student should practice safe sex abroad.

Behavior and conduct

Your student will be subject to the laws of the host country. Sometimes these laws might be very different from what they are used to in the United States or carry more severe punishments. In most cases, the host university will outline expectations around student conduct, and students who are in violation could be sent home at their own expense.

Drugs and alcohol

Your student should be aware of local laws and social norms pertaining to drugs and alcohol (e.g., lower legal drinking ages, criminalization of marijuana usage). Your student might be tempted to use study abroad as a time to experiment. Instead, encourage your student to know their limits, attempt to understand the cultural context, and always be aware of their surroundings when going out with friends.

Money and banking

Be sure your student has a small amount of the local currency on hand when they arrive. This can be obtained at a currency exchange kiosk in an international airport. Your student should inform their bank and credit card companies of the locations and dates they will be traveling, so the bank does not suspect overseas charges to be identity theft and freeze the account. In addition, investigate policies around international transaction fees and exchange fees. Encourage your student to use only official and legitimate ATMs during the day and with a buddy. If your student is traveling for a semester or more, follow the recommendations of their provider on whether or not to open a local bank account.

Transportation

Public transportation is usually a very affordable and reliable means of getting around, encouraged over renting cars or a moped. However, students should be aware of potential dangers caused by lax safety regulations, inconsistent adherence to traffic laws, and crowded hubs where tourists can be easily spotted and taken advantage of. Research trusted local ride-sharing companies, and take only official marked and metered taxis.

Communication

Many students find it simple and cost-effective to purchase their cell phone carrier's international plan while abroad. Others may choose to purchase local SIM cards. Free Wi-Fi is abundant in most major cities, so messaging apps like WhatsApp, Signal, and Discord might be a great way to stay in touch with your student.

Making the Most of the Experience

As your student adapts, they may begin to wonder how to make the most of their experience. Here are some intentional things your student can do to make the most of their program abroad, even if it's only a week long.

Personal

Attempt the local language. Your student doesn't need to be fluent or have formally studied the local language; just the attempt will demonstrate respect, curiosity, and effort that will open doors to deeper relationships and interactions, which will in turn provide greater insight into the culture.

Developing relationships with locals is another way to maximize the travel experience. Your student will be tempted to spend most of their time with the other Americans they are traveling with, and for good reason. Powerful bonds are created between students who experience such monumental transformation together. However, local relationships provide significant cultural understanding and create a local support network. Your student can forge these friendships by developing daily or weekly routines like visiting the same café or library, volunteering in the community, or joining sports and clubs offered by their host institution.

Many students insist on maximizing their experience by visiting every major tourist attraction. The history museums, art galleries, and religious architecture are important, but some of the most fun discoveries come from everyday experiences. Shopping at the grocery store, waiting in line at the post office, or observing kids on their way to school can reveal great cultural insights, because these familiar experiences are easy to relate to and put things in perspective. Resisting the urge to document every single experience can help your student appreciate and live in the moment.

Academic

Study abroad is a great way for your student to take courses they couldn't get at their home university, learn from global thinkers, and get a new perspective of their discipline. One of the biggest shocks students experience when they study abroad is the difference in the academic environment. Classroom norms like discussion, group work, and workload can be very different from what a student is accustomed to. To succeed, it is first important to attend class! This seems like a no-brainer, but it can be tempting to ditch class regularly to travel on long weekends. Next, encourage your student to develop connections with faculty members at the host institution. This will help them build social capital, so when problems do arise, the faculty member is more likely to help. It is important that your student reaches out to the study abroad provider and takes advantage of resources available like tutoring, disability services, etc.

Professional

Many students are able to maximize their study abroad experience by advancing their career goals at the same time. It can be challenging to gain professional work experience abroad because of language barriers, visa restrictions, and local labor laws, but some study abroad programs allow for internships, job shadows, or informational interviews. Study abroad is a great time to network and make international contacts. It also helps your student practice cross-cultural communication.

If your student has considered living or working abroad after college, this is a great time to explore the nuances of an international job search. For example, in some countries, job seekers submit a curriculum vitae (CV) instead of a résumé, and it might be customary to include personal information on that CV, like a birth date or photo. Your student could explore how locals become aware of job opportunities, what role interviews play in the process, and what office culture is like.

Visiting Your Student

While your student is abroad, you might be tempted to visit. In most cases, study abroad providers welcome family visits, but there are a few important factors to consider:

- **Select dates with care.** Plan to travel with your student before their program starts, after their program ends, or on a scheduled academic break to minimize interruptions to coursework or activities. Meeting your student at the end of their program has special advantages: They will have the inside scoop about the best attractions and will be better tour guides!
- **Inform the study abroad provider about your intention,** and ask if they can help facilitate your visit. They might provide you with guidelines and even provide recommendations for accommodations and activities.
- **Plan for your own housing.** Whether it's a dorm, homestay, or apartment, it is likely that your student is in a living environment with other students, making it inappropriate for family or outsiders to stay in those accommodations. Look for a hotel or hostel nearby.

- **Avoid joining courses, excursions, or tours that are part of the program** and designed for students. The study abroad providers are managing budgets, travel logistics, and safety guidelines that could be disrupted by your involvement.

Returning Home

When your student returns, it is likely they will experience reverse culture shock, with a roller coaster of emotions as they attempt to reacclimate. At first, they may be really happy to see everyone they missed, but then they may feel lonely or bored, missing their overseas friends or routines. Giving your student a chance to reflect on their experience is a great way to help them adjust. Ask to see pictures or help them create a scrapbook. When you can understand how profoundly impactful their time away was, they will feel less isolated. Encourage your student to keep in touch with the people they met. Help your student incorporate their new perspectives and habits into their everyday life at home, like adopting recipes or sustainable habits from their host culture.

Many students cope with reentry by planning their next trip. If your student was bitten by the travel bug, there are many ways they could go abroad again. Your student's study abroad office can direct your student to some of these opportunities and assist them with their applications.

- **Study abroad again.** Many students find a way to study abroad more than once, especially if they can maximize financial aid to help them do so.
- **Apply for international fellowships.** Fully funded international activities, like the Fulbright U.S. Student Program, pay for recent graduates to spend several months to a year abroad to do research or a project, teach English, or attend university abroad.

- **Look at graduate school.** Universities abroad are locally accredited, can be prestigious, and often cost a lot less than graduate school in the United States.
- **Work and volunteer abroad.** There are many programs that help students live and earn money abroad. In addition to the Peace Corps, for example, the JET (Japan Exchange and Teaching) program allows you to teach English in Japan, and BUNAC (British Universities North America Club) helps young people secure youth visas to work and volunteer abroad. Your student could seek out jobs with international companies and request transfer to their overseas locations.

What if Your Student is the One Staying Home?

If your student doesn't have the ability or has chosen not to study abroad, it's possible to feel left behind. The fear of missing out can be exacerbated by seeing pictures and videos of a friend's adventures on social media or by noticing the disruption of routines if friends are absent from campus. This can result in feelings of loneliness or jealousy. There are a few strategies your student can try in order to minimize the impact of their friends' departure:

- **Make new friends.** Work to expand friendship networks by creating new social habits.
- **Try new experiences.** Try something new, such as an internship, joining a research team, starting a club, or participating in a domestic service learning trip.
- **Focus.** Improve grades or participate in leadership on campus.
- **Think positively.** Be excited for friends and recognize that each is doing what is best for them at this moment. If

international travel is something your student wants to do in the future, their friends who studied abroad will make great tour guides!

Closing Advice

The most obvious outcome of your student's study abroad journey will be confidence. After weeks of problem-solving and challenging themselves, your student might think, "If I can do that, I can do anything." You will be amazed at how they have blossomed, and hopefully you will feel like a small part of their success because they truly couldn't have done it without you.

> ### Conversation Starters
>
> - What is the most interesting thing you've learned so far about the country/city/culture?
> - What are you missing about home?
> - Have you made any local friends? Tell me about them.
> - What will you miss the most when you return?
> - What have you learned that you want to incorporate into your life when you return?
> - What is one challenge you've overcome that you are most proud of?
> - What is something you've learned about yourself in this process that has surprised you?

Chapter 7
YOU WANT TO DO MORE SCHOOL?

How to support the decision to attend graduate school

Shanise N. Kent, Esq., MBA
University at Albany, State University of New York

Chelsea Petree, Ph.D.
Rochester Institute of Technology

After completing four or more years of college, you may expect your student to say they are done with exams, papers, and presentations and have no interest in any more education. In today's market, however, obtaining a graduate degree may not only be the best option, but also required. Graduate school, like undergraduate education, requires both financial resources and time. Your student should go to graduate school if they have a passion for learning, if they want to specialize in a specific area, if it is required for their intended career, and/or if it will allow for additional professional growth. Start having conversations with them about the benefits, considerations, and process. If your student plans to enter graduate school immediately following completing their bachelor's degree, they will need to plan early to take required standardized tests and submit their applications on time. Even if they plan to take time off, thinking about it during their junior year can be beneficial as they consider references, paths, and programs.

Benefits

There are many benefits to attending graduate school following a bachelor's degree.

Higher earnings; lower unemployment

Graduate school can lead to more earning potential, as salaries tend to increase for each degree earned, though students should take the cost of attendance into consideration. Additionally, education beyond the bachelor's degree often results in lower unemployment.

Getting noticed

Even if it's not required in your student's chosen field, an advanced degree could set them apart. A bachelor's degree alone can fail to get applicants noticed in a job search when other candidates have a graduate degree. It's not just about the education itself, but the lessons and skills students learn as they complete a master's or doctoral degree. A graduate education provides a deeper level of understanding in a specific field, and also professional skills and maturity that do not always develop at the undergraduate level. This often shows up on résumés and in interviews.

Deepened knowledge

A graduate degree allows students to pursue their interests in more depth. Most undergraduate degrees have course requirements outside of a student's major, which is hugely beneficial at the bachelor's level. A graduate program allows students to focus on their field and choose a specific area of study that will become their specialization.

Preparation for the future

A bachelor's degree sets students up for success. A graduate degree can make success easier to come by. Graduate school opens your student's network up in incomparable ways. Faculty often have connections across the field. As graduate students form closer relationships with professors, they are more likely to link into this invaluable network. Graduate school also provides more hands-on experiences than bachelor's degrees tend to. Through research, teaching, writing, presenting, or working directly with companies, students gain professional experience and are more prepared to work in the field when they graduate.

Considerations

While there are many benefits, there are also important considerations that your student needs to think about before making this decision.

Commitment

Whether your student wants to do a two-year master's degree or a six-year doctoral program, a graduate degree is a big commitment. It is not just more school, and a student thinking it will be just like their undergraduate years needs to reconsider. The coursework at the graduate level will be more rigorous, often requiring extensive reading before class sessions. Students work with far less guidance or supervision from their professors, and they will be expected to work independently and thrive on their own. To be a successful graduate student, they need to think of it less like school and more like a job.

Focus

Graduate school is not necessarily the time to explore areas of study. Students should not apply directly out of their undergraduate degree as a way to figure out what they want to do or because they don't know what's next. This is a waste of time and money. They should also not use graduate school as a way to delay getting a job. They should have a solid idea of what they want to do and the area of the field they want to focus on as they apply.

Cost

Finances should be a top consideration when thinking about graduate school. If your student has strong undergraduate credentials (e.g., a good GPA, undergraduate research experience, related work experience), they may be excellent candidates for graduate-level funding. This funding can include a full tuition scholarship and living stipend in exchange for working up to 20 hours per week as a research assistant, teaching assistant, or administrative graduate assistant. Additionally, there are external fellowships that students can apply for at the graduate level that would include tuition scholarships, living stipends, and additional financial assistance (to cover fees, travel, and health care, for example). Finally, there are need-based grants and scholarships, as well as student loans for graduate students. Some employers will cover tuition as part of their benefits package, which is something to consider.

Advanced Degree Options

Your student will need to determine what type of degree they will pursue. In the American educational system, the first graduate-level qualification is the **master's degree**. Master's degrees can be research-intensive (e.g., master of arts in political science) or designed for professional preparation (e.g., master's in social work). Research-intensive master's degrees typically require coursework, seminars, comprehensive exams, and defense of a master's thesis. Professional preparation master's programs may require coursework, seminars, internships, and capstone projects. Master's degree programs are typically one to two years in duration.

The highest academic qualification in the United States is the **doctor of philosophy** (PhD), which is a research doctorate degree. A small fraction of students pursue a PhD each year; those who do typically want to become college faculty, establish careers in research or policy, or become clinical psychologists.

Professional degrees, such as doctor of dental surgery (DDS), doctor of dental medicine (DMD), doctor of medicine (MD), or juris doctor (JD), qualify students to enter a profession. All professional degree programs are closely regulated by recognized accrediting agencies.

Choosing a Graduate Program

Identifying programs to apply to can be quite the research project, and your student should plan to devote considerable time to this activity. Your student can narrow down their list by:

- Reading program descriptions and promotional materials
- Attending graduate fairs
- Speaking with undergraduate faculty, current graduate students, or alumni
- Visiting campuses

Program rankings and selectivity can help your student make a realistic assessment of their chances of being admitted. Yet, decisions on which programs to apply to should not be based on rankings and selectivity alone, because there are many other factors to consider.

If your student is applying to a research-intensive program, they should narrow their list by determining whether there are faculty members with research interests that match their own. Your student should investigate each program's curriculum, and determine whether the primary emphasis suits their career goals, whether the program offers specializations, and whether there are cooperative programs with other educational, cultural, and research institutions available. Compare the facilities of each prospective program. How extensive are libraries, laboratories, and computer facilities? Are there specialized research facilities? Do the programs offer or require internships, practicums, or clinical experiences? What are the demographics of the graduate student body, how many students will be in their entering class, and what is the attrition rate (the rate at which students drop out of the program prior to completion)?

Applying

A graduate school application will typically consist of three parts: the application itself, letters of recommendation, and a personal statement.

Deadlines

Whether they are applying through a centralized application service or to programs individually, your student should review all application requirements and make a list of deadlines. Deadlines can be as early as November of senior year. Often, the more competitive the school, the earlier the deadline. Your student should apply as early as possible within the application period. To be considered for funding, they may need to apply earlier than the standard deadline. Some programs may review applications on a rolling basis, and submitting early may give the applicant a leg up. Your student should become familiar with all instructions and pay attention to details.

Letters of recommendation

Most graduate applications will require up to three letters of recommendation. Encourage your student to make a list of potential letter writers, focusing on securing recommendations from their faculty. Ideally, your student will schedule appointments with the reference writers to discuss programs of study and schools of interest, as well as skills of the student that the writer may want to highlight. They should give their writers four to six weeks to write the letter.

Personal statement

In preparing their personal statement, or statement of purpose, encourage your student to be direct, honest, and sincere. Admissions committees are interested in an applicant's clarity of research interests (if applying to a research-intensive master's or PhD program), unique story, steps they have taken to prepare for graduate education, and short- and long-term goals. The admissions committee also wants to know why its university is the applicant's top choice and what the applicant knows about its program's focus.

Standardized testing

A fourth part of the application process, which is becoming optional in some cases, is a standardized test. The type of graduate program will determine the standardized test needed (e.g., LSAT for law school, MCAT for medical school, GMAT for business schools, GRE for general graduate studies). If your student intends to go into graduate school immediately following graduation, the ideal time to take these exams is during the spring or summer *before* their senior year. Scores are valid for three to five years (depending on the test) if they want to take it but continue to explore postgraduate options.

Timing

Perhaps your student is interested in graduate school but wants to take a little break. Taking a break can be beneficial. Graduate school is not something you want your student to jump into if they are unsure about what they want to study or where they want to go. Finding a program that is a good fit and completing applications can be time-consuming, and it may be difficult to put the right amount of effort in while completing senior year. With the additional level of work and maturity needed for graduate school, time off is in the best interest of many students.

If this is what your student wants to do, help them make a plan, including the following points:

How long will they take off?

After working hard to graduate with their bachelor's degree, it is completely understandable if your student needs some time off to recoup and reenergize. The trick is to not take so much time off that they lose sight of their goals. Once they start getting a regular paycheck and get into a new (exam-less) routine, it can be hard to find motivation to fill out those graduate school applications. Remind them, however, of their long-term goals. It is always easier to go back to school sooner than many years down the road.

If your student knows they want to pursue a graduate degree but decides to take a year or two off after they've already been accepted, many graduate programs will defer admission for a year. Encouraging your student to apply to graduate school, jobs, and other postbaccalaureate opportunities in their senior year will give them the widest set of options to choose from after they complete their bachelor's degree.

How will they make the most of their time off?

There are a number of ways graduates can prepare for the next step. If earning money is a priority, they shouldn't stress too much about what kind of job they get. If they will work an outside job while going to grad school, a job with flexible hours or part-time options could be beneficial. Saving during this time will allow your graduate to worry less about finances when they return to school.

If they want experience in their field but cannot find a job, volunteering is a great option. Along with the formal programs offered for graduates (e.g., Peace Corps, AmeriCorps), students can see if there are volunteer opportunities within the graduate program they hope to apply to or in a similar field at another university. This will give their application an added boost when they go to apply, and it will open up new networks and reference options.

Closing Advice

Graduate school is an excellent option for any field, and a necessity for many. Attending is not, however, a decision that should be taken lightly. Getting an advanced degree is not "college: part two." Students should be prepared for a higher level of thinking, work, and academic involvement, but also for great rewards and opportunities.

Conversation Starters

- Why are you considering graduate school?
- What field would you want to pursue an advanced degree in?
- Which programs have you started considering and why?
- How would graduate school support your career options?
- How will you prepare for the shift to this new level of education?

Chapter 8
CAN I SEE YOUR ID?

How to talk about turning 21

Ahmed Hosni
The Ohio State University

The college experience promises to have a profound impact on your student, inside and outside the classroom. Decisions about nutrition, sleep hygiene, finances, relationships, and time management will impact their success on campus, as well as their transition into a profession after graduation. Some of the most important decisions students may face while at school will be regarding alcohol. These will present themselves almost immediately after a student steps onto campus and continue throughout their time in college. During high school, many students already began shaping their values and beliefs around alcohol use based on their own experiences drinking or through witnessing its impact on their peers and family. These beliefs and values will be challenged often when on campus, and students will begin to experience different forces pulling them toward the age-old question:

To Drink, or Not to Drink?

It is a question as old as time. Alcohol has had a significant role in society for thousands of years, playing a pivotal role in the coming-of-age process. This is especially true in today's culture, where drinking while young, especially during college, is normalized and seen as part of being a student. The reality is much different than what we see in movies, where students are depicted as regularly inebriated, overindulgent, and making questionable decisions regarding alcohol. Instead, we know that for all the teenagers who may lean into the stereotype of the drunken college student, there are students who are making healthy decisions when they do drink, and many who are choosing not to drink at all. It can be helpful to understand what forces are impacting these decisions.

The College Environment

Many students begin their college journey with preconceived attitudes and beliefs around drinking, developed through behavior modeled by parents and family, peer influence, and societal and cultural influences. Now on campus, students will be faced with the decision to drink regularly. They will see peers navigate the decision to drink, and many students will associate the decision to drink with fitting in, making friends, and having an increased sense of belonging. For 18- to 24-year-olds, fitting in can be a powerful motivator. Other factors that influence drinking is how readily available and inexpensive alcohol is on campus. The ease of access makes the decision to drink much easier than it should be for underage students, as most campuses are surrounded by businesses whose focus is to sell alcohol to such students in bars and stores. We are also in a time where high-quality fake IDs are easy to find. This means that turning 21 is often not when a student goes to purchase a drink for themselves for the first time, a milestone of past generations.

Peer influences on drinking

It is easy to get distracted by the bright lights of campus bars and clubs, the music resonating from the parties off campus, and to convince oneself that going out and drinking is what everyone is doing. The reality is that, on any given night, most students are *not* drinking. Yet, the perception for many students is that most of their peers *do* drink. This makes the decision to drink much easier, even for students whose values and beliefs about drinking may have prevented it up to this point. Social acceptance and sense of belonging are some of the strongest motivators for college students, and the behavior of their closest peers are some of the greatest influences they will have.

Traditions and culture

While most campuses share some features that influence drinking, like easily accessible alcohol and the fact that alcohol plays a role in the social landscape, there are a few factors that increase the rate of alcohol misuse. There are many schools that have traditions associated with alcohol. This is especially true for schools that have large sports traditions. The students at these schools tend to drink at higher rates than schools that don't have large sports cultures. The same is true even for the students at those schools who don't identify as sports fans or attend sporting events. Similarly, participation in a fraternity or sorority increases the amount of alcohol a student consumes. Students affiliated with Greek organizations have been shown to have adverse consequences related to alcohol consumption even after they've graduated.

You might ask yourself:

- Did your student rush a fraternity or sorority? If so, have you seen a change in their academic success or behavior?

- Did your student choose a university that has a significant sports tradition? If so, has tailgating and attending athletics events become a regular part of their experience?

These students are likely facing decisions regarding high-risk drinking on a regular basis. Remember that many are making good choices and, for those who make decisions that negatively impact them, they often learn from their mistakes, especially when they have caring relationships and people who support them.

Living arrangements

Where a student lives also impacts the amount of drinking they will do. Of all the college living situations, those living at home with their parents typically drink the least. Next are the students living in a residence hall. Those who live off campus without their parents drink the most and have the highest rates of problem drinking. The number goes up even more if the off-campus housing is in a fraternity or sorority house.

Because most colleges require students to live on campus their first year, and many now also require a second year of living on campus, the increase in drinking associated with moving off campus has become more aligned with third-year students and turning 21. This is due in part to the lack of supervision from parents or residence hall staff and being able to drink at home without consequence, possibly for the first time. As students enter their third year of school, they will want to find living arrangements with people they like and in a building they enjoy. Consider:

- Do you know your student's friends at school, especially those they may be choosing to live with? It is likely they will have a huge influence on your student's health, well-being, and success.

- Has your student considered remaining in the residence hall rather than moving off campus? Explore the options of remaining on campus and seeing if there are unique housing options for third- and fourth-year students.

Many schools allow students to apply to be residence hall advisor, which makes the cost of living much more affordable and also provides opportunities to grow and develop as leaders on campus.

For students who end up in their own place off campus, it is important they understand their responsibility to do what they can to keep friends and partygoers safe if they host a party. Having clear guidelines for their guests is important. It is also important to maintain a guest list and try to stick to it. If not, the party may get out of hand. Being a responsible party host will be as important as making healthy decisions.

Turning 21

Despite the accessibility of high-quality fake IDs for college students, the 21st birthday is still a monumental moment. No more worrying about being caught with a fake ID or having to memorize names, birth dates, and addresses of strangers or made-up people. For students who haven't used a fake ID, it might mean their first time going to campus bars and feeling like a real adult. But what about the student who will have to wait longer for their moment to evolve from green underclassman to elder statesperson on campus? This can be a difficult adjustment period for those who are forced to continue attending house parties and pregaming while their friend group has moved on to barhopping and concession stands. Being the last in your friend group to turn 21 can pose significant challenges to one's sense of social belonging, especially if alcohol plays a large part in your group's social life.

Supporting your student through this time might look like encouraging them to lean into their hobbies and interests outside of activities that include drinking. Does your student have any friends who don't drink? This could be a time to strengthen those relationships. A potential pitfall to avoid is starting to attend parties with individuals they don't know well. Having a friend group your student knows and trusts is important when going out on a college campus.

Conversations About Healthy Decision-Making

Helping students make the best decisions for themselves should be a team effort, though the student has to be open to the conversation and is ultimately responsible for their actions. University staff and faculty often play a pivotal role by providing students with the knowledge and skills they need to make informed decisions around drinking, and for suggesting strategies they can use to make sure that when they do drink, they do so safely. Parents and families have been doing this work for many years, whether through having meaningful conversation, modeling healthy decision-making regarding alcohol, or instilling values which prioritize safety and responsibility. As your student becomes more and more independent, the influence you have doesn't diminish, it only changes. Research shows that parents and families continue to be some of the most important influences in a college student's life through school and after graduation. As your student evolves and develops, so should your relationship with them. Here are some suggestions for having conversations with your student around healthy decision-making:

- Connect with your student. Set a regular day and time that you chat about how things are going.
- Become a trusted person so your student wants to share their struggles and seek advice from you. You can ask for

their advice, which will demonstrate what the new dynamics of your relationship might look like.

- Remind your student about the laws regarding alcohol use in their area and of the consequences of breaking those laws.
- Model healthy decision-making for your student, which includes not driving while intoxicated, drinking in moderation, and showing positive behavior while drinking.
- Remind your student how proud you are of them when they display healthy decision-making. If they are struggling with healthy decisions, be the firm and trusted support they need to get back on track.

Another important conversation to have with your student is about your family history with alcohol. For many families, alcohol plays an important role in their traditions, like holidays and family dinners. These occasions are what help shape your student's understanding of safe drinking and the positive role alcohol can play in their life. For other families, alcohol misuse is a part of their family history, even when it doesn't occur in their own household. This information is important for individuals making decisions about whether to drink or not, because alcohol-related problems, especially alcohol-use disorders (also known as alcoholism), can be inherited. This background can help your student make smart decisions and help them to be alert if alcohol begins to have a more prominent role in their life.

College-Specific Behaviors Associated with High-Risk Drinking

High-risk drinking is common on college campuses; there is no way around it. When students move off campus and begin spending more time in spaces that aren't monitored, those behaviors become riskier and happen more often. Here is a list of these high-risk behaviors:

- Drinking alcohol under the age of 21
- Chugging drinks, not measuring shots or liquor, and/or participating in drinking games
- Drinking something without knowing what it is or where it came from
- Drinking to get drunk
- Drinking and driving
- Mixing alcohol with medications, energy drinks, or illegal drugs
- Drinking to fit in
- Engaging in sexual behaviors while intoxicated

The good news is that all of these behaviors are avoidable. Here are some tools and tips to help students avoid high-risk drinking:

- Create a plan. Ask yourself things like, "How much will I drink? How much will I spend? What time do I need to head home? How will I get to and from my destination safely?"
- Alternate between alcoholic and nonalcoholic drinks.
- Have a buddy system. Go out with friends who have similar values and beliefs about drinking and be accountable to one another. Don't go home without each other.
- Never leave a drink unattended. If you go to the bathroom, have your friend hold it. If you lose sight of it even for a minute, it's time to get a new drink.
- Eat before, during, and after you plan to drink. Also, drink plenty of water before, during, and after.
- Don't drink when stressed. It can often lead to overconsumption and create more stress and problems than you had before.

- Understand campus resources. Many schools have something called a Good Samaritan policy, which encourages students to contact university staff if they notice an individual who has passed out or shows signs of serious effects from alcohol or drug consumption. These policies typically protect the caller, the person in need of assistance, and any witnesses involved from receiving disciplinary sanctions.
- Know the answers to these questions: What will you do in case of an emergency? Does your campus have a Good Samaritan policy? If something happens to you or someone in your group, who will you call?

Closing Advice

Decisions around drinking are going to be a part of the college experience for most students. Making healthy decisions around alcohol, including drinking in moderation or choosing not to drink at all, can make the experience at school much better for your student. As they navigate this part of the experience, try to be someone they can be open with rather than fearful of your response. Openness will allow your relationship with your student to evolve and make sure that you continue to be an important voice in their life.

Conversation Starters

- How will you make the decision to drink or not to drink when the opportunity arises?
- What are some things you do to relieve stress that don't involve drinking?
- Do you know what to do if someone at your house or a party you attend has had too much to drink?
- Does your school have a Good Samaritan policy?
- Now that your friends are 21 and you still have some time, what else can you do to have a good time that doesn't involve going out?

Chapter 9

THERE'S NOT AN OFFICE FOR THAT?

How to advocate for resources after college

Samantha Jeffries, LMFT
Rochester Institute of Technology

College, in and of itself, is a period of transition. Each year of your student's education brings new challenges and steps toward their next phase of life. Junior year is a time during which many students begin to dip their toes into what life will be like in the "real world." They are still in the protective bubble of college, but they may begin to explore resources outside campus, such as off-campus living, off-campus medical providers, or community connections through various local activities. Now is the time, while their safety net is still in place, for them to discover what support and resources they need not just to be successful in their academics, but to be successful after college as well.

As a parent, it can be difficult at times to create space for your student to figure things out independently, while also providing advice (sometimes from a distance) about what to expect when the safety net of college is gone. It can also be difficult to encourage your student to connect with resources that you didn't know existed, never needed yourself, or didn't know they needed. There will be moments when your student seems to have a great road map for how to navigate life outside college, and other moments when your student just doesn't seem to "get it." This chapter will lay out some of the common resources available to college students, what will change when they graduate, and how to encourage your student to use this year to really build their ability to self-advocate.

Common College Resources

Let's begin with a few quick disclaimers. At this point in your student's college journey, you are likely aware of most, if not all, of the resources below. The intent of this section is not to continue educating you about resources that you learned about back in your student's first year, but rather to highlight the need to help your student engage with these resources now and to think through how these common resources will be different after college. Many of the resources will be referred to as "free." While we, as parents and professionals, know that the supports offered through a college or university are, in fact, not free and are paid for by tuition and fees, most students often don't make that connection. It can be helpful in your discussions with your student to remind them that this is one of the few times in their lives when the cost of large resources will be bundled together, often at a much cheaper rate than they will be outside college. Many of these fees that are bundled into tuition are also mandatory, so take advantage of what has already been paid for!

Living

Perhaps one of the most common amenities that comes to mind when thinking about college life is **housing**. Often, students can overlook the fact that living on campus comes with some additional perks such as resident assistants (RAs) and numerous layers of residence life support. If they have a roommate conflict or a room concern, for example, there are supports in place that they won't have off campus. Residence life staff can mediate roommate conflicts, assist with locating new spaces to live on campus, or provide support getting connected to the larger campus community. Students also don't have to worry about setting up and paying for utilities or convincing a landlord to complete repairs and waiting for that work to be done.

While **dining** on campus can receive mixed reviews, it is yet another amenity that students often overlook. Eating on campus allows students to have a variety of options to select from without having to grocery shop and cook for themselves. Students sometimes refer to their meal plan as "fake money," and in some regards that is accurate. Their meal plan is money that is designated for food, and, therefore, they don't have to sort through and budget what money needs to go toward other living expenses versus what they will use to eat—it's already determined for them. Additionally, dining services often employ registered dieticians who can meet with students to assist them with dietary concerns and creating meal plans that best fit their needs.

Health/Wellness

Student health services (e.g., primary care providers, mental health counseling) are often available to students right on campus, allowing students to access care without having to locate providers in the community. While these offices can sometimes have a cost associated with them (usually through a health fee that is attached to a student's bill), the benefit of having access to services without having to sort through health insurance, transportation, and provider availability is yet another amenity that students are often unaware of. If your student needs a flu shot, for example, they do not need to worry about calling their doctor, scheduling an appointment, driving to the office, and covering any appointment co-pays; often they can just attend a flu shot clinic on campus. Most of the time, fees associated with access to health services are mandatory, so this is one of those resources that students have already paid for. Use the services while they are "free!"

Case management is relatively new within higher education settings, so it is likely not a resource that many parents and families are aware of from their own time in college. Case management can serve many functions within different college settings, but one of the primary services offered by this office is assistance with resource navigation. A case manager can help students understand resources that are available to them on and off campus, how to connect to support services, and how to navigate more complex personal problems. Say your student needs assistance finding a medical specialist in the community who accepts their health insurance. A case manager can help with this. Or your student is struggling to understand which supports on campus are appropriate to connect to (because there are often so many!). A case manager can assist with this as well.

Remember the days when you could sleep in and get that workout in at any time of the day? Even better: You weren't bothered by the nagging guilt of having paid for a gym membership that you might not be putting to good use. Welcome to college, where the **gym and fitness classes** are, you guessed it, FREE! Often, students don't realize the high cost of a gym membership in the community, and they certainly don't understand that the more specialized the gym, the higher the fees.

Academics

Disability services is another resource available to students in need of short- or long-term accommodations (e.g., physical, academic, mental health). Your student can connect with someone who will help create reasonable plans to make college academics and living more accessible and supportive of whatever their needs may be. It is important to note that, while the support of disability services on campus is free, costs associated with a particular accommodation (e.g., equipment) will be passed on to the student.

Is your student struggling with creating their academic plan? **Academic advising** is available to provide support throughout your student's college experience. An advisor's primary role is to support your student through their academic journey and assist them with creating the best path to graduation. Advisors are also able to connect students to free tutoring resources on campus, should your student need additional assistance with a particular class.

Career advising is available at universities to assist students with résumé building, locating career opportunities on and off campus, and gaining job interview skills as they begin job searches. Career counselors are also able to chat with students about what careers might interest them and the steps to take now to succeed in those careers.

The library is an easily overlooked free resource. As a student, you don't realize the cost associated with certain scholarly articles or books, and that's because your college has already paid the fees. Most libraries even have programs where they will locate a book at another institution and have it shipped right to you. There is a world of knowledge at your student's fingertips and at zero additional cost.

What Changes in the "Real World"?

It is no surprise that many of the supports put in place for a student during high school and college eventually disappear. One day your student may call you and say, "I can't stand my roommate, and I hate my apartment." Well, welcome to the real world, where you now have a legally binding lease! It is important for your student to understand that, once they begin to leave the safety net of college, many of the resources they are used to having become significantly less accessible. Nobody is going to host a resource fair. They now must choose what resources they need, prioritize budgeting to cover the cost of those resources, and actively work to connect to them. It may also really shock your student to learn that there are many supports they are accustomed to having that don't exist for them now. For example, there is no Individualized Education Program (IEP) for the workplace.

In an ideal world, your student would be prepared for the changes they are facing as they transition from college into adulthood. Many students have experimented with apartment or off-campus living, and they are well-versed in grocery shopping, cooking for themselves, budgeting their finances to cover expenses, and working with a landlord. However, this is not a uniform experience across the board, and many students struggle with the lack of support and resources once they graduate.

During their college years, students can draw on student loans and/or family support to cover living expenses. After graduation, student loans are no longer accessible and family support may greatly decrease, so students must learn to rely on their own income to cover expenses. Locating and obtaining affordable housing that fits a budget can be a challenge, one made greater when landlords require first and last month's rent in addition to a credit check (and most college students don't yet have great credit).

Suddenly, they no longer have access to the medical and mental health care they were receiving on campus and must learn how to use their health insurance to connect with community-based providers. Students who were previously accessing lower-cost health insurance through their university may need to obtain health insurance coverage before they can even begin the process of connecting to community providers. Need to access care quickly like you did in college? Waitlists abound in the community, and students must work to understand the medical system and what supports (e.g., urgent care, primary care, hospital) to access in certain times of need. And, unlike in college when they could connect to a case manager for help navigating these complexities, students no longer have a one-stop office they can visit for assistance.

As students move into the workforce, they may realize that this is yet another adjustment to their support system. Students who were connected to frequent tutoring may find that they need to seek more frequent supervision and outside training for their jobs, which may or may not be available. Accommodations once obtained through disability services now become a matter for human resources, and extended time on work might not be offered. Additionally, not all employers or states offer the same benefits when it comes to short- or long-term disability, and, while human resources assists employees with navigating these concerns, the process in the workplace is often significantly more complicated than needing some time away from class.

Encouraging Students to Advocate for Themselves

So how do you help prepare your student for this next step? It can sometimes feel like you have spent years working on preparing them for adulthood, only to realize that there are some things that can only be taught in the moment. How often have you tried to talk with your student about what comes next, only to get the "yeah, yeah, yeah" response? While it may often seem as though your student doesn't understand what they want or need, the fact is they usually know exactly what they need. They just don't know that help exists to get them there or how to look for it. Once they have found someone who can help, they then have to use the skill of advocating for themselves, which can be intimidating. You can't prepare your student for everything, but you can help your student learn to identify their needs and then to advocate for them.

As parents and professionals, we know that nobody can identify your needs (and express what would help you the most) as well as you can.

In your younger years, though, it can be difficult to say to someone, "this is what I need," or even, "this is how I am feeling." For example, it can be intimidating to ask your employer for some extended time on a task because you have a lot going on in your personal life, or to ask a roommate for some help around the apartment or to chip in more money for expenses. Encourage your student to practice direct and open communication. As hard as it may be to come right out and say what you need, the worst that can happen is that you don't get what you are asking for. Here are some tips you can pass onto your student when you talk about direct communication:

- **Practice verbal and written communication in advance.** Give yourself some time to gather your thoughts and ensure that you are sharing everything you intend to share.
- **Ask questions.** Just because we are taught to trust people in positions of authority (e.g., your doctor) doesn't mean that you cannot and should not ask questions to help clarify concerns.
- **Be an active listener.** Sharing our thoughts and feelings is only half of good communication. It's important to actively listen to help create an open-minded environment and to ensure that we are fully understanding what is being communicated.
- **Practice using "I" statements.** "I think," "I feel," and "I need" decrease defensiveness in communication by reducing blame, while highlighting how things are impacting you.
- **Monitor your tone.** It can be easy to get caught up in the heat of your feelings, but remember that if someone is turned off by *how* you are speaking, then they aren't paying attention to *what* you are saying.

Remind your student that sometimes the outcome of a conversation is not what we wanted or expected, but that doesn't mean that we don't listen, accept what we must, and continue advocating for ourselves when needed.

Closing Advice

Talk with your student about the resources available, the resources they may need, and how to locate some of those resources outside the campus community. Help them think about how they can transition some of those supports and resources into life after college. Talk about how your student might leverage their strengths to get what they need.

> ### Conversation Starters
>
> - What resources have you used during your time at school?
> - What resources/supports do you anticipate needing outside of college?
> - How can you find a medical provider in the community?
> - Can you explain to me how leases and utility bills work?
> - Can you explain the difference between a credit and a debit card? Which do you have?
> - Do you have any questions for me about life outside of college?

Chapter 10

IS THIS RELATIONSHIP SERIOUS?

How to navigate increasingly romantic relationships

Christine Self
Texas Tech University

Your student's dating relationship may deepen during their junior year, and that can be difficult for them (and you!) to navigate. With increasingly busy schedules, making time for a significant other can be challenging, but it is a part of adulthood. You may wonder just how serious your student's romantic relationship is. You also may question the amount of time they spend with their partner, especially when it encroaches on your time with your student during school breaks. This chapter will share information about what a junior-year relationship might look like and tips for how you can talk to your student about their relationships.

How Serious Are They?

As your college student embarks on their junior year, you might notice a shift in their priorities and, chances are, dating and relationships are climbing up in the ranks. Juniors have solidified their footing in school but are also beginning to think more seriously about life after graduation, including who they may be spending their post-college journey with.

While the thought of your student settling down might make you nervous, don't worry. Most young adults aren't rushing down the aisle until their late 20s or early 30s. Nevertheless, dating relationships start to become a more significant aspect of students' lives as they move through college. Many juniors take dating relationships quite seriously, and relationship troubles often find their way into students' conversations with college mental health professionals.

On the other hand, the infamous hookup culture, the online dating scene, or the societal pressure to embrace their upcoming senior year as a wild ride may encourage your student to avoid serious relationships and have fun their senior year, so it's important to be aware of those external influences as well.

Sometimes, students see their impending graduation not only as a time to celebrate their achievements, but also as a time of uncertainty in their lives. They may see graduation as a threat to their relationship with a significant other who has different postgraduation plans or who is younger than them and staying behind. Students may even change their minds about graduate school plans or where to live after college based on their significant other's post-college intentions. Talk with your student about their goals and aspirations. Try to listen and offer advice without interfering or pushing too hard for *your* vision of their post-college life.

Managing Competing Obligations

It's only natural to be concerned about the amount of time your student is investing in their significant other, especially considering the more intense and major-specific classes they're taking now.

Adding the time investment of a deepening romantic relationship to an already-crowded student's plate can feel overwhelming, but recognize that succeeding in academics and maintaining a rewarding relationship are both important aspects of your student's life. As adults, we read and hear a great deal about the importance of work-life balance, and that applies to college students' lives as well. Talk to your student about managing stress and finding time to enjoy themselves with their significant other while also meeting their academic goals.

The concern about your student's time goes beyond academics. You may find yourself wondering about the impact of a serious dating relationship on the time spent with your family versus with their significant other and their family. With limited holidays and time off, the question of who gets to spend Thanksgiving with their family can become a delicate issue. Resist the urge to engage in a tug-of-war with your student's significant other for their time. Rather than competing, consider offering options and being flexible. Understand that your junior is navigating a complex period of growth and exploration, and their personal relationships are an integral part of that journey.

Encourage open communication and discuss holiday plans well in advance so that everyone is on the same page. Perhaps alternating holidays with each family or celebrating occasions on different days would work. Your flexibility, support, and understanding can foster a sense of security for your student, helping them manage their time effectively without feeling torn between competing obligations. The need for flexibility with holidays will continue throughout your student's adulthood, and starting now will set the stage for the future.

Remember that your junior has a lot going on. Helping them find a healthy balance between academics, personal relationships, and family relationships is a difficult, but not insurmountable, task, and your openness and encouragement can help.

Recognizing Unhealthy Relationships

Hopefully, if your junior is in a romantic relationship, it's a positive one that is based on mutual respect. However, some relationships are unhealthy, and it's important for parents to be vigilant about the potential warning signs of unhealthy relationships.

Keep an eye out for signs like things moving too fast, intense and overwhelming emotions, manipulation, sabotage of other relationships, isolation from family and friends, belittling, and volatile behavior. If you notice any of these warning signs, it's time to talk to your student.

Approaching your student about their relationship can be tricky, but it's crucial. If you are in a healthy relationship, share your experiences openly. Discuss what makes your relationship work and ask open-ended questions about theirs. Inquire about their mutual interests, the evolution of their relationship, and what they enjoy about their significant other. Building a bridge with communication is key.

If these conversations lead you to suspect that your student is in an unhealthy relationship, be there for them in as nonjudgmental a way as possible. Talk directly, openly, and honestly with them about your concerns. This can help create a safe space for open dialogue, allowing your student to share their thoughts and feelings with you. Use questions such as:

- What do you like best about your partner?
- What are some things you enjoy doing together?
- What makes you feel connected to your partner?
- How does your partner show you they care about you?

If you do see red flags in your student's relationship, don't hesitate to refer your student to campus resources like the Title IX office. These professionals are equipped to provide supportive measures and assistance to help your student cope with the challenges of an unhealthy relationship. Encourage your student to seek help, and let them know that reaching out is a sign of strength, not weakness. Reaching out for help is often one of the most difficult things a student experiencing relationship difficulties can do, so emphasize what an important step it is.

As a parent, your role is not to interfere with your student's relationships, but to observe, offer guidance and support, and empower your student to make informed decisions. If your student chooses to stay in an unhealthy relationship despite your conversations, continue to provide support and a listening ear so they feel comfortable coming to you when they decide it's time to leave.

Not Dating? That's Okay.

In today's world, some people are waiting longer to engage in serious relationships and get married. More people are staying single and choosing not to marry at all. Your young adult's journey may not mirror your experiences, and that's perfectly okay. Gone are the days when marriage was a milestone achieved in the early 20s. The trend has shifted, and today's college students are not diving into adulthood at the same pace you might have. Many are navigating the complexities of higher education and personal growth, focusing on establishing their individual identities before committing to serious relationships. If your junior isn't showing interest in dating, don't worry. They may simply not be ready for serious relationships. Times have changed, and the dating scene is now influenced by myriad factors that might differ from your past.

Moreover, your student may be dating but choosing to keep this part of their life private. In an era where personal boundaries are prized, some students prefer to navigate the nuances of relationships away from the eyes of their parents and extended families. They may fear judgment or discomfort, especially if they have not come out to their families about their sexuality. Create an environment of trust and openness. If your student isn't ready to share details about their dating life, respect their privacy. Foster a space where they feel comfortable discussing their experiences when they're ready.

Understanding that your junior's journey may differ from yours is the key to providing the support they need. Embrace the uniqueness of their path, whether it involves dating or not, and offer guidance and acceptance as they navigate the complexities of relationships in their ever-evolving college life.

What About Friends?

For your college student, friendships can be just as crucial, if not even more so, than dating relationships. By the time they reach their junior year, many students have solidified a core group of college friends, a support system that might endure for the rest of their lives. As with dating relationships, students may see their future graduation from college as an ending of time spent with people dear to them and have mixed feelings about the occasion.

On the other hand, you may be concerned that your junior doesn't seem to have many close friends. Some young people thrive in social circles, fostering connections with a multitude of friends, while others forge one or two close-knit bonds. Some may even prefer a more solitary path, keeping to themselves as they navigate the challenges of college life. Remember that it takes time to make friends. For some students, deep friendships like the ones they formed with childhood friends could take years. Focus more on connections. Does your junior know where to go to spend time with others who share common interests? Recognize and respect your junior's approach to friendships.

Of course, if you are concerned about feelings of loneliness or isolation in your student, reach out to campus resources that can help, such as the student counseling center, for advice. Ask how to refer your student to their office if you feel it's warranted.

College is a time of exploration, and friendships play a pivotal role in shaping your junior's experience. By acknowledging and supporting their unique social journey, you contribute to their growth and well-being during these transformative years.

Closing Advice

Though your student is maturing, they still need your guidance. Talking to your college junior about dating and personal relationships may seem incredibly awkward, but one of the great things about juniors is that they're becoming more mature, gaining a solid foundation for their academic careers, while also beginning to think about their futures. That maturity and focus on the future should make conversations about serious dating relationships easier. Having open, honest conversations will help them feel safe confiding in you should anything go wrong. Watching your college student grow and forge relationships that may last a lifetime can be incredibly rewarding for your entire family.

Conversation Starters

- Are you serious about [person's name]? Do they have similar life goals as you? How do you know?

- How do you feel your relationship with them is progressing? Are things going too fast, too slow, or just right?

- Are you getting enough time to yourself to manage your classwork, interests, and extracurricular activities?

- When it comes to the holidays and other family time, are they as open to spending time with us as you are to spending time with them? How should we approach the holidays so that you get to see everyone you want and still have some time to relax?

- What are they planning to do after graduation? How would you feel about living in different places while you each work on your post-college plans?

- Am I putting too much pressure on you about dating? Is there anything you'd like to ask me about dating, or do I need to give you more space?

- Are you spending enough time with friends and peers? If you're feeling isolated, let's think through some ways you might make more connections with others this year.

Chapter 11

HOW CAN MY CHILD TRANSITION FROM STUDENT TO CITIZEN?

How to engage in the off-campus community

Joshua Lee
St. Olaf College

For many college students, junior year represents a significant turning point. It's often the time when they're allowed to move off campus and begin trading in the familiar (and sometimes limiting) comforts of the campus bubble for the exciting world outside it. Exploring the surrounding community may seem like a small step, but these junior year privileges can usher in a wave of new learning moments and invaluable life lessons. This chapter will describe how your student's world may be expanding as they gain independence off campus, explore new personal and civic freedoms, and initiate healthy habits for their future.

Exploring Life Off Campus

One of the most common privileges of junior year is the ability to choose off-campus housing. While parents may view this as just more responsibility, it is an exciting opportunity to learn new life skills.

Consider how infrequently students are required to complete the fundamental tasks of homeownership. Students come with varying degrees of experience in this area, but this may be the first time your student will:

- Sign a lease or rental agreement
- Change a fire detector battery
- Budget for monthly utility bills and living expenses
- Negotiate expenses with roommates
- Resolve roommate conflicts without the help of a resident advisor
- Restart the pilot light on a furnace, water heater, or fireplace
- Reset a GFCI outlet or fuse box

While it may be tempting to swoop in and help your student with these firsts, remember that learning these life lessons firsthand will better prepare them for the future.

Living expenses

One life skill is of particular importance—budgeting. While many students have high salary expectations for their first job, it takes time to earn that desired income, and a steady paycheck after graduation is not guaranteed. So, for many juniors, this is the time to learn how to live on a limited budget when income is already scarce. If your student has not created a monthly budget, now is the time to start, regardless of how much money they have or how they earn it. If your student has a part-time job, encourage them to map out how they plan to spend their money before it is deposited into their bank account. If you are largely funding your student's living expenses, consider depositing a set amount into their account on a biweekly or monthly basis to encourage them to budget their funds as if they had a job.

Discussing finances can be sensitive, but encouraging these habits now is important. If you are covering your student's living expenses, clearly outline what those funds cover and identify your expectations. Students who have a clear understanding of the costs of their education and living expenses will be better prepared to make personal and professional decisions. There are many resources available to assist you in this conversation. Most major banks have tools to track and categorize spending. There is also a plethora of phone applications that can help with budgeting and even assist with splitting bills with roommates. Another option is to reach out to the financial aid office on campus to request budgeting resources or to seek out educational seminars.

Recreational expenses

Once living expenses have been covered, encourage your student to budget for recreation. Not only is budgeting for recreation important for personal wellness, but finding recreational activities can also become a valuable test of resourcefulness. Campus events can become predictable by junior year, so exploring budget-friendly activities outside campus can be an adventure in itself. It may be as simple as finding local festivals without an entry fee, taking note of venues with student discounts, or coordinating a group of friends to go on a road trip. Whatever your student chooses to do in their free time, encourage them to plan ahead for these activities.

As your student takes steps toward more independence, you will experience a range of emotions, particularly if they choose to spend holidays elsewhere. In these situations, try not to feel slighted. Give them space and encouragement to take advantage of these moments in a safe and healthy way. If you have preferences about certain family gatherings, communicate your expectations early, and don't assume your student has the same understanding. This is a time when social bonds strengthen. Students want to express themselves and experiment with what they enjoy and who they enjoy their time with. These social connections will foster relationships that are the cornerstones of a fulfilling life. Many can attest to the fact that making friends is more challenging in the "real world," so why not take advantage of a moment when most of the people around you are in the same place and stage of life?

Giving Back, Gaining Purpose

In the relentless pursuit of good grades and career preparation, community service can feel trite or, at the very least, like obligatory résumé fodder. However, community service can have transformative power and build personal growth. It can also lead to unexpected career connections and lifelong friendships.

Service opportunities are available in every community. Some can be found by searching volunteer websites like volunteermatch.org, and others can be found by approaching organizations directly and offering time and talent. There are a variety of campus resources to get your student going in the right direction, including the student activities office, student volunteer groups, or national service fraternities such as Alpha Phi Omega (APO). Joining a national organization like APO is not only a great way to find service opportunities, but reputable organizations will also be recognized by employers all over the world.

One of the benefits of community service is character growth and soft skills. While the classroom is an excellent place to gain theoretical and technical understanding, service opportunities challenge students to do unfamiliar tasks and use problem-solving skills to resolve real-life issues. When students select organizations that align with personal passions, their time becomes even more purposeful. Experiences gained as a volunteer integrate into their lifestyle. Students who dedicate themselves to regular service can't imagine life without it, and they effortlessly develop the practical skills employers look for.

Finally, community service work inevitably fosters new connections and exposes students to local challenges. Working toward solving local issues will build a sense of community in a way that academia often doesn't. Service opportunities offer a sense of purpose and fulfillment that extends beyond academia and professional pursuits. Encourage your student to explore their passions and interests, even if they are not directly related to their major. Volunteering may not create immediate career gains, but it will open doors to new ideas and relationships. Time and time again, alumni point to their volunteer involvement as the single most rewarding part of their college experience because of the difference they made in their communities. Students can take this sense of civic purpose with them regardless of where they live next or what job they hold.

Becoming a Responsible Citizen

One of the fundamental expressions of citizenship comes in the form of voting. While junior year may not be the first time your student has voted, it is likely the first time they are weighing their decisions in ways that feel independent of their family. Using their academic lessons to navigate real-world problems, registering to vote, finding a polling place or submitting an absentee ballot, and actively advocating for issues they care about are all important life skills.

As students interact with a diverse community of students on campus, there is no doubt that their worldview will evolve. That evolution manifests in their voting choices and what issues they choose to support. While this can become an inflection point between students and their parents, take time to listen to what your student engages in and how their values are being challenged or reinforced. If politics becomes a particularly contentious topic, create some ground rules that establish an appropriate time and place for dialogue.

Registering to vote and finding a polling place is a great summer conversation before the academic year begins. Primary elections and general elections can easily be overshadowed by deadlines and other academic demands. Does your student want to vote in their *home* state/city or their *college* state/city? They should do a little research about what or who is on each ballot and then look into residency laws, which vary by state. Check out ALL IN to VOTE (allintovote.org) or visit the NASS (National Association of Secretaries of State) website (nass.org) to learn more about residency requirements.

In addition to reinforcing your student's right to vote, there are other ways to get involved as well, particularly for international students or those who have not reached the age of majority yet. Participating in student government, writing to local representatives, speaking to their city council members during public comment, joining a political organization, and engaging in civil discourse on campus are all concrete ways to translate classroom knowledge into tangible action.

Ultimately, we all benefit from an informed democracy. While we may not agree on everything, civil discord is crucial for responsible citizenship. College campuses are prime locations for political and values-based discussions. When the opportunity is right, ask your student how or what they are learning about issues that impact their campus, community, and beyond. It is a small step, but we can all contribute to modeling respect, civil dialogue, and our freedom to voice our opinions at the ballot box.

Closing Advice

As your student takes steps toward more independence, it's natural to feel a mix of emotions. You might feel excited for them, but you may also feel concerned or even a little disconnected. At this point in your student's academic career, there is still plenty of time for them to explore. The path to responsible adulthood is paved with learning experiences, both successes and stumbles. While managing your student's experience is not recommended, gentle nudges here and there can go a long way to ensuring your student is making progress toward healthy lifelong habits.

> **Conversation Starters**
>
> - How do you plan to spend your breaks this year? Are you planning to come home or try something new?
> - How are you handling living on your own?
> - What are some unexpected issues you've come across with your housing?
> - How are you managing your bills with your roommates?
> - Have you considered getting involved with something off campus in the community?
> - Have you registered to vote yet? Do you know where/how to vote?

Chapter 12

IS MY STUDENT SENIOR READY?

How to make the most of junior year

Ashley Boltrushek
American University

Summertime between junior and senior year is fast approaching for your student. They, and you, are likely to be flooded with questions about how they should best spend their time, and this chapter is here to reassure you that there is no right way or one path to prepare for the final year of college. Junior year is full of possibilities, and your student will determine what feels best for them. So, how can you help them thoughtfully consider options rather than doing what they assume they *should* be doing?

Self-Care and Self-Reflection

How is your student investing in themselves and those around them? Incorporating time for self-care and restorative practices is important now and for establishing good habits in the future. Self-care prioritizes their well-being and helps them to better take on difficult circumstances. Whatever the method (e.g., via a hobby, volunteer activity, exercise, vacation), what are the components of those practices that help bring balance to your student? Acts of self-appreciation do not have to be elaborate and expensive to be meaningful. For example, making coffee for yourself every morning can be self-care. Ask your student what little things bring them joy and how they incorporate these into daily life.

How are they approaching summer and what do they believe they need to set themselves up for success? Planning for postgraduate fulfillment is important, of course, because they've been working toward this for years, but is that planning what they most need right now? Each discipline has its own set of classes, expectations around engagement with internships, and skills needed to enter into their field professionally. All of these components—blended with who your student is as a person, the identities they hold, skills they've refined and are developing, how they learn best and approach their work, and what they derive their strength and motivation from—will contribute to finding the best path forward for summer.

Postgraduate Plans

Is your student interested in applying to graduate programs? They should look closely at the requirements for each program, specifically entry exams (e.g., DAT, GMAT, GRE, LSAT, MCAT, PCAT, TOEFL) and minimum scores required for entry, writing samples or portfolios, application costs, and number and types of recommendations.

Is your student interested in working full time? They should look closely at the job description—specifically responsibilities of the role—supervisory line, entry-level experience required, compensation, growth opportunities (e.g., funding for certifications, webinars, structured learning in the role), and work hours.

Is your student interested in volunteering full time? They should look closely at the organizations, types of opportunities (e.g., AmeriCorps, City Year, Peace Corps, Teach for America), where in the world (literally!) they could be, language/vaccination/training requirements, stipend amount, and cost of living coverage.

Everyone contributing to this book understands the stress that comes with deciphering the alphabet of entry exams, applying for jobs, and finding rewarding volunteer programs, but not even one of us did it alone, and neither will your student. No matter the path they choose, your student will become more autonomous, refine their skills, and develop new ways of connecting to others. Encourage your student to seek out conversations with faculty and staff. Every campus landscape is slightly different, but your student has access to career and academic services, health and well-being resources, diversity and inclusion offices, community service, student activities, and spiritual life teams—and they are all there to help.

Summer Prep

So how does your student get organized and minimize the strain related to these processes? Even for the proudest of procrastinators, having a little proactive structure to keep on task will be important. Whatever method(s) your student is willing to use to organize themselves is perfect, and helping them be accountable to their (realistic) deadlines will go a long way. Some of the most tried-and-true strategies include:

- **Do the hardest thing first.** In this context, perhaps the hardest thing is having an honest conversation with your student about what they *want*, not what *they think they should do*. Reserve time and energy for the things that matter most.

- **Body double.** Being present with one or more people who are also working on completing tasks can help get things done.
- **Create a comprehensive to-do list.** Sure, your student can brain dump all the things they need to do into a spreadsheet or planner, but formulating action steps for each item and batching tasks will make the most of their time and energy. It will also give you an easy way to help them celebrate their progress.
- **Practice self-care.** Yes, I am mentioning it again! Our brains and bodies need time to recharge, but sometimes taking breaks seems antithetical to getting things done. Give your student a boost through encouraging breaks, snacks, and movement.

General Considerations for Success

Here are some questions to ask before guiding your student in discussions about what may come next.

What makes your student feel happy? Motivated? Energized? Balanced?

Harder classes are calling during junior year, and they'll likely be more interesting to your student topically, but also more demanding. Encourage your student to find balance with their remaining courses and avoid pushing classes off until the last semester or front-loading everything right now. If your student is unsure how to develop a well-rounded course schedule, suggest that they schedule an appointment with their academic advising team. Just as incorporating self-care brings restoration, your student's brain needs a break. Ask them to consider taking one class that, through its modality or topic area, is the opposite of their course of study. Stretching the mind in a different way can bring space for the parts being exercised the most.

***What makes your student hesitate? Concerned?
Worried? Exhausted?***

Anticipating changes of any kind, even the ones your student has been wanting and waiting for, brings a shift of understanding, of environment, and of the way they've been doing things. It requires them to carve new pathways. Embolden your student to (re)discover the things they've had access to during the past few years. What are the clubs, organizations, friends, coffee shops, spaces on campus, or local haunts that your student has come to appreciate? Which are the ones they've left unexplored? When your student reflects on the past few years, the places and people that have anchored them will be important to relish. Invite them to appreciate what these have meant and the memories they've made and want to make before they step away from campus.

***What is your student losing? Grieving? Missing?
Soon to be without?***

In this context, I'm not talking about grief in the *capital G* sense of severe loss or hardship, but the grief we all manage daily. I ask students to frame loss of any kind as an opportunity for healthy self-reflection and reconciliation; in this way, grief is an easily understood feeling to use when navigating these changes. Your student is preparing to leave their undergraduate career, and this will be a significant loss. They might be leaving some of their favorite things behind them. Even if they continue to have access to these places and people, the relationship to these things is no longer the same, and that transition matters.

As your student approaches senior year, what stands out to them most? What are they already sad to be without? Opening this dialogue with your student can be meaningful as they get ready for their final year of college. Encourage your student to ask these questions of friends across campus, share memories, participate in activities together, and ask each other how they're feeling and what they're looking forward to for the year (and beyond). In the same way that each student will approach their summer planning process differently, they'll also evolve through their final year differently. It's not too late for your student to make the most of their remaining time as an undergrad.

The First Last Year

Your student is entering into their first last year—let that sink in. All the hard work, time, energy, excitement, tears, successes, mistakes: Your student is more resilient now than when they began their first year. Everything they have done up until now has helped them thrive. They will continue along that path, but you can help them by being prepared for the occasional roadblock and detour. This first last year can impact your student's behavior in ways you (and they) did not anticipate. Will they pull further away from you or cling more closely? Will their communication style shift and, if so, how will you feel reassured that your student is getting what they need? Normalize this process for them; all these behaviors are part of the process of loss and transition.

The enormity of what senior year can be is daunting. For some, the pressure is completely on and can feel insurmountable, while others remove all sense of pressure. Your student should aim somewhere in the middle of that sliding scale, knowing that it will ebb and flow during the course of the year. Remind your student that what they are doing—going to class, doing their work, talking to friends—all matters, but they may not matter equally at all times.

Closing Advice

Ask your student the questions you are curious about. Ask them how they are spending their time and what they are gaining from it. Remind them that spending time with peers during college is just as important and meaningful as spending time studying. Remind your student that, on this shortening road to graduation, there is still time to slow down, be present, and center themselves in their experience. Self-care and what works this year (for you and your student) might not be the same as what has worked before. Help your student try new ways of being present for themselves in this final year. You have managed major transitions before, too, and have grown from them. How can you relay that knowledge and growth to your student, even if the circumstances are not the same?

Most importantly, parents, your student will always be your baby, but they are a bit more grown now. They got this. And you got this. And when it feels like maybe they *absolutely, most certainly do not got this,* remember that we are here to help you all, too.

Conversation Starters

- How are you feeling about approaching your final undergraduate summer?
- What is giving you pause or hesitation about the end of your college career?
- What is bringing you joy and balance?
- How do you plan to make the most of your final year in college?
- What deadlines or requirements do you have to consider this year to prepare for post-college life?

Conclusion

Through the questions, challenges, and stress, junior year is special and should not be rushed through. Juniors are confident in their knowledge of resources and college life. Classes may be more challenging, but they are also more interesting. It's exciting to look ahead to life after college, while also enjoying the opportunities and amenities they still have access to. By the end of this year, your student will have not only made progress toward their future, but they will also have lasting memories of their college experience.

More and more each year, you will see your student become an adult. Their independence will increase, and they will need you maybe not less, but differently. While you may occasionally miss the days when they needed you for every little thing, embrace the adult they are becoming and the freedom you have in not having to manage every aspect of their life. Remember that they do still need you and want you to be a part of their life. Let loose, embrace their independence, and look ahead to the final year of this college journey.